# HOW TO
# INHERIT
# MONEY

*A Guide to Making
Good Financial Decisions
After Losing Someone
You Love*

By
Michael Alexander

CAREER PRESS
3 Tice Road
P.O. Box 687
Franklin Lakes, NJ 07417
1-800-CAREER-1
201-848-0310 (NJ and outside U.S.)
FAX: 201-848-1727

HOW TO INHERIT MONEY
ISBN 1-56414-350-3 $14.99
Cover design by Rob Johnson
Printed in the U.S.A. by Book-mart Press

To order this title by mail, please include price as noted above, $2.50 handling per order, and $1.50 for each book ordered. Send to: Career Press, Inc., 3 Tice Road, P.O. Box 687, Franklin Lakes, NJ 07417.

Or call toll-free 1-800-CAREER-1 (in NJ and Canada: 201-848-0310) to order using VISA or MasterCard, or for further information on books from Career Press.

**Library of Congress Cataloging-in-Publication Data**

Alexander, Michael, 1956-
    How to inherit money : a guide to making good financial decisions after losing someone you love / by Michael Alexander.
        p.    cm.
    Includes index.
    ISBN 1-56414-350-4 (paperback)
    1. Inheritance and succession.    2. Inheritance and transfer tax.
3. Finance, Personal.    I. Title.
HB715.A43    1998
335.024--dc21                                                    97-44081
                                                                      CIP

# Acknowledgments

Almost three years ago, my business partner, Patrick Graham, and I were talking on the phone one evening, musing over the great advantages and disadvantages I had experienced in receiving a major inheritance when I was barely a teenager. I suggested that a fitting title for the film version of my life story would be "How to Inherit Money and Live to Tell About It." In the same moment, I realized I had the coined the title for my first book. Within the next month, I had written a proposal for a self-help guide for inheritors, and eventually signed a deal with HarperCollins.

In the course of my research and writing, my primary concern was to ensure that every chapter would be relevant to the needs of any inheritor. So I sent a draft copy of each chapter to people from various walks of life, who provided valuable criticism and advice. Among others, included in my sample group were a university professor, a legal secretary, a fund-raiser, an artist, a figure skating coach, a nurse, a film producer and a psychiatrist. I offer my heartfelt thanks to the members of this group, all of whom I recognize in the following list, for their encouragement, support and willingness to make time to assist me: Patrick Graham, Maya Mavjee, Willie and George Fennell, Rick Myers, Bill and Helen Dimitroff, Dave Wex, Ken and Paulette Ormsby, Rev. Gardiner Dalzell, Dr. Taras Babiak, Dr. Mary Vachon, Miles Kronby, Stuart Coxe, Dore Potter, Lynne Gallagher, Kathleen Kelly, Cliff and Donna Orwin, Robert Paul, Randy Friedland, Barbara Dick, Malcolm Burrows, Wodek Szemberg, Paula Absolon, Bill Eigles, Adrian Lee, Carol Lee, Mary Lee, Jim O'Donnell, Ralph Hicks, Len Kubas, Victoria Taylor, Sybil House, Bob Buckberrough and the late Louise Rousseau.

I also owe special thanks to Bill Graham for his unflagging support of my business and literary endeavors, Sheldon Teicher for his timely legal advice and Michael Levine for taking an interest in my writing at an early stage and using his formidable business and legal skills to help me find a suitable publisher.

Needless to say, mentioning these people in no way indicates their agreement with the ideas contained in the book.

*...whosoever looketh into himself, and considereth what he doth, when he does think, opine, reason, hope, feare, &c, and upon what grounds; he shall thereby read and know, what are the thoughts, and Passions of all other men, upon the like occasions.*

—Thomas Hobbes, *Leviathan*, 1651

# Contents

# Foreword

As a psychotherapist who has worked with people confronting life-threatening illness and grief for more than 25 years, I know how valuable Michael Alexander's book, *How to Inherit Money*, can be if you will let yourself be open to its lessons.

Perhaps you are someone who has recently confronted the death of a loved one and are turning to this book to understand what you are experiencing and to receive advice on how to handle your inheritance. Maybe you received an inheritance a while ago and have experienced many conflicts as a result. You can't figure out what went wrong—why you made some decisions that in retrospect appear to have been poor. Or perhaps you can't explain why you are no longer talking to family members with whom you were once close. Maybe you are confronting a life-threatening illness and want to understand the grieving process so you can plan your will and minimize the problems your family and friends will have as they deal with whatever you are leaving them: money, the family silver, a home, jewelry or your precious stamp collection.

On the other hand, you may be healthy and very health conscious but want to plan your will and disbursements in the most sensible way; you hope to help your family members avoid some of the problems that grief may bring. Or you may be in the health, medical, mental health, legal or financial planning professions, wishing to gain some knowledge to improve your understanding of what your clients are experiencing.

Whatever your reason for reading this book, I can promise that it has many insights. Mike Alexander learned his lessons about inheriting money the hard way and he has many experiences to share with you. He will help you understand how judgment may be "profoundly and surreptitiously distorted by grief." This includes understanding the symptoms of grief, such as depression and self-confusion, and the secondary losses associated with death. He also shows you how to recognize when you have sufficiently overcome the symptoms of grief and are ready to make important decisions.

If your inheritance has left you affluent, or feeling affluent compared to your previous life style, Mike will help you understand the resulting problems you might experience and, hopefully, avoid making some of the mistakes made by others. If you have made mistakes or feel that mistakes were made by other family members or experts in handling the estate, this book will help you to understand what went wrong. You may find that you had unresolved issues with the person who died, with your own identity, with your role in the family, or with the role of another person. Perhaps there were long-standing family dynamics that were invisible when the person was alive, but that surfaced after his or her death.

Some of the insights you will gain may be painful. Personally and as a therapist, I can tell you this is often the case with the most important lessons we learn in life. Most of us learn some of our most difficult lessons from grief, but our reaction to it can be helped by understanding its dynamics, sharing our feelings and opening ourselves to receiving practical help from the right people. You must be careful, as Mike warns, not to treat a trusted friend as an expert or an expert as a trusted friend when it comes to issues of handling your inheritance. I think, however, that in reading this book you will come to see Mike as an expert, and may even see him as a friend. He will help you to inquire into the ultimate meaning of loss in your life—a loss that has already happened or that you anticipate in the near future, or your anticipation of your family's experience of losing you. He urges you to seek the right advice and gives practical assistance to help you find the right balance between personal and professional advice.

In his warm style, Mike draws on and shares his personal experiences, many of which were very difficult. His hope is that by using his own experiences and insights he can help you avoid some of the difficulties that he encountered. Through his use of case studies from his consulting practice, the lay press, philosophy and literature, Mike will help you understand a lesson from *Hamlet:* that for those who suffer from extreme grief, the self-insight that leads to sound financial judgment is attained by taking the time to examine and answer fundamental questions about the purpose of life itself. Sometimes financial wisdom is acquired only by acquiring wisdom itself.

From my work over the past quarter-century with those facing their own deaths and with grieving survivors, I know many people who would have profited from reading this book. I hope the wisdom Mike shares with you will help you develop your own wisdom and avoid many of the pitfalls that others have experienced.

—Mary L. S. Vachon, RN, Ph.D.

Consultant in Psychosocial Oncology and Palliative Care, Toronto–Sunnybrook Regional Cancer Centre/Sunnybrook Health Science Centre

Associate Professor, Departments of Psychiatry and Behavioral Science, University of Toronto

Clinical Consultant, Wellspring

# A Note Concerning Case Studies

As a consultant who also holds two law degrees, I must at all times maintain the confidentiality of my clients' affairs. When a colleague comes to me for advice on behalf of his or her client, I owe that client the same duty. And, as a matter of course, I extend the privilege to friends and acquaintances when they seek me out to discuss financial and personal matters.

The duty of confidentiality created an obvious problem for me during the writing of almost every chapter of *How to Inherit Money*. The only way to illustrate my arguments effectively was to use case studies drawn from the experiences of clients—mine and others, the predicaments of friends and stories related to me by colleagues. And yet my position required me to protect the privacy of these same people.

My solution was to practice benign subterfuge. I changed key facts, transposed particulars and developed fictional characters. While my own experiences are related factually, all the others, save the ones taken from newspapers and magazines, are a careful blend of fact and fiction designed to obscure the original situation while preserving its underlying truth.

........................

# Chapter 1

# The Inheritance Generation

I had my first experience with grief and money when I was 13 years old. On a dreary Sunday afternoon in March of 1969, my mother decided to indulge my favorite pastime. She took me for a car ride around the streets of our little city of Chatham, Ontario (population 35,000), in my grandfather's Rolls-Royce. As we cruised the main boulevard, where muscle cars had left a trail of skid marks the night before, my mother turned our conversation toward my grandfather's recent illness. He had been in and out of the hospital for the past year and a half and, after some surgery, seemed to be in good health. (After all, during a recent trip to the local cigar store, I had overheard him tell the shopkeeper, "By Jove, I've never felt better.") I was crushed as my mother slowed the car to a snail's pace, turned toward me and gently broke the news: The doctors were giving my grandfather another two months to live. I couldn't say a word. I stared at the Spirit of Ecstasy perched atop the grille and felt my stomach twist and turn.

On April 16, 1969, my grandfather died in the Public General Hospital. Eleven days after my 13th birthday, I suddenly became an heir to a fortune. I had no idea on that terrible day that this inheritance, which everyone in our community would celebrate as my great advantage in life, would eventually become a great burden.

My grandfather had been the leader of our family. (My mother and grandmother were his only other immediate survivors.) He had been larger-than-life, a self-made man, who had built his own radio station in the early part of the century. (It was one of the first privately owned stations in North America). His insight and business acumen had made him financially independent. Like most self-reliant people who had achieved success in the 1920s and 1930s, when the state wouldn't lend a helping hand if you fell down, he was adamant about controlling his own destiny. In the family, this meant he played the role of patriarch. He made all the financial decisions, was reluctant to share his business secrets and doled out money when he saw fit.

We had been utterly dependent on his good will and success. Now we were lost. He had failed to prepare us for the difficult transition that followed. Money became tight after the state took almost half his wealth and crooked agents pilfered some of his accounts. My mother, a professional musician, and my grandmother, who had spent her life serving her church, charities and social clubs, did their best to cope with their new financial responsibilities. But when all was said and done, I was the one left in charge of my grandfather's estate.

I was forced to become a teenage executor. At 16, I became the caretaker of various possessions. In my late teens, I learned how to read estate accounts, stock quotations, and legal documents. By the age of 20, I was meeting with lawyers and trustees on a regular basis to discuss legal and financial issues and was largely responsible for administering the estate, which included a trust fund and an art collection.

During the next 10 years, I enjoyed the privileges of this position, mostly by pursuing studies in political science, philosophy and law. At the age of 30, I was about to enter a graduate program at Columbia University that would allow me to launch a teaching career. But, at that moment, my life was turned upside down. In August of 1986, my grandmother fell ill with an incurable pancreatic disease; one week later, my mother was diagnosed with breast cancer. For the next year, I remained in Canada and attended chemotherapy sessions, maintained vigils outside operating suites, sat for countless hours in hospital rooms and arranged for ambulances, nurses and homemakers. My grandmother went quickly, passing away in January of 1987. However, by the summer, my mother appeared to be improving. As a result, she insisted that I accept Columbia's offer and move to New York, a step that I took reluctantly. My hesitation proved to be a harbinger. By the end of the first semester her condition had worsened and she died early in the new year.

My mother's last request was that I carry on with my studies, but in the months following her death, in the throes of extreme grief, I could barely sleep. Writing a thesis on Kant's political and legal philosophies was out of the question. Eventually I had to take a leave of absence from Columbia to regain my sense of well-being and deal with my inheritance.

I was suddenly saddled with huge financial responsibilities again. I alone would be responsible for liquidating and winding up my grandfather's trust, my mother's estate, and my grandmother's estate. Over the previous 17 years, I had learned how to manage a collection of fixed and stable assets: residential real estate, blue-chip stocks, bonds, antiques and automobiles. Now, as sole beneficiary, I would have to make difficult decisions about which assets to keep and which to dissolve, which to store and which to use, which to hold for sentimental reasons and which to hold as investments, which to retain for interest income and which to reinvest for higher yields. I would have to pass judgment on the worth and utility of three lifetimes of investments, possessions, papers and mementos. With ready cash, I had to face another set of difficult decisions: Should I invest for capital gains or increased income? Should I set up a retirement fund, invest in a home or speculate on the stock market? To deal with these issues, I would have to acquire new business skills and learn more about my own aspirations and needs.

I was forced to drop everything to deal with these emotional and financial problems. At the time, I thought I could handle everything. Since I had been involved in the management of family money for years, and now had the advantage of a law degree, I assumed I could deal with this wealth (or at least find the people who could deal with it for me) and quickly return to school to complete my program. I turned out to be wrong on all counts. I made many mistakes in administering these three estates. In some cases, I defied rules of management I had been practicing successfully for over a decade. And I paid a price for it. I took losses on assets, dissolved possessions I should have kept, and made investments that were incompatible with my personal goals. When the dust finally settled, I realized my judgment had been profoundly and surreptitiously distorted by grief.

In what follows, I want to tell you about the many problems I faced in trying to manage my inheritance, in particular how grief prevented me from making sound financial judgments. My hope is that other members of my generation, many of whom will receive an inheritance from parents or relatives, will learn something from my experience. Given that so many younger North Americans have had to accept lower standards of living due to a series of punishing recessions and slow growth over the last 20 years, the key to living well for many of them will be learning how to manage an inheritance successfully. One aim of this book is to advise them on how to do that.

The most important advice I hope to convey is that you must finish grieving the loss of your parent, sibling, relative or friend before deciding what to do with your inheritance. This applies to an inheritor of any age. Only when you have overcome the disfiguring power of grief can you make financial decisions that are based on a clear understanding of your real needs and aspirations. (This, by the way, might mean waiting a year or two before making fundamental decisions about the management of your inheritance.)

Much of what I want to tell you is drawn from the experiences of friends, colleagues and clients who have come to me for advice on how to deal with their own inheritances. My education in estate matters made me a valuable source of information for others. They came to me for both legal and personal advice. The legal questions were often very straightforward. For example: Do I have to pay a capital gains tax on the family home? Do I have to declare my mother's jewelry for tax purposes? As executor of my brother's estate, what kind of powers can I exercise? And so on. The law provides pretty clear answers to these questions.

After discussing some of these issues with heirs, I found that they all faced painful personal dilemmas in trying to decide what to do with their bequests.

- "Should I keep the family home, even though it's located 200 miles from my current residence?"

- "Should I hold on to grandmother's silver collection? It meant so much to her, but tea parties don't really fit in with my life style."

- "My mother left me a retirement fund that can't be touched until I'm 65. At 40, with two kids headed for college, shouldn't I collapse the fund and use it to help my family today?"

- "My sister is so upset. My father left me in complete control of the family business, but she's the one with the business degree. Should I go against my father's wishes and give her a piece of the company?"

Most of all, these people wanted to know how to deal with these difficult personal questions. A lawyer can't really answer them. They can be answered only by considering, among other things, what you really value, how you want to live in the future, what you wish to preserve for your own children, what role sentiment plays in your life; in other words, they can be answered only by knowing yourself. When the most important issues must be resolved through personal insight, you're better off seeing a minister, a therapist, a wise old uncle or taking long walks in the country than consulting a lawyer.

While I often advised people to seek counsel on personal matters elsewhere, frequently I found that they wanted me to share what I had learned from my own struggles with inheritance. After a while, I was giving personal advice most of the time. I did so with a good conscience for one simple reason. I had discovered that one of the most difficult aspects of inheritance was finding someone competent to advise on these tough personal issues. I spent months talking to lawyers, accountants, financial advisors, stockbrokers, and family friends as well, looking for some good advice on how to arrange my bequests to complement my life.

Let me tell you something: I'm still trying to recover from all the bad and contradictory advice I received. Some of the worst advice came from professionals who were leaders in their fields. One accountant advised me to collapse a protected investment fund without telling me about the future tax advantages of holding on to it. One of my trustees negligently failed to advise me about a potential capital gains tax on a major asset. A long-time family friend and trusted expert in the field of real estate drastically overestimated the value of my family home to convince me to let him sell it. An antique specialist urged me to sell my grandmother's most valuable art objects because they weren't tasteful (later I learned that real collectors found them very tasteful indeed). Some close friends exhorted me to sell all the family possessions and start a new life ("You'll have to be ruthless," one said). Others chastised me for thinking of letting anything go.

From all this "good advice," I learned one very important lesson: A lot of people give pretty bad advice when it comes to inheritance. Some people are just out to cheat you. Others, particularly close friends, are sometimes too confident that they know what is best for you. High-profile professionals, on the other hand, are often too busy to take the time to consider the long-term consequences, or the personal consequences, of their advice. I received the best legal advice from small-town attorneys who already knew me, or took the time to get to know me, and offered advice with caution, realizing they didn't have all the answers to the world's problems or mine.

So, when people come to me for help, the first thing I do is issue warnings about personal advice. Then, I try to make them think about what is best for them, not for me or anyone else. My aim is to make my clients think twice or even three times before making a serious decision about the management of an inheritance. Most of all, I try to warn about the power of grief.

In case you're wondering how I made out, I did eventually find a way to profit from all of my bad experiences with inheritance. After returning to New York to complete my program, I had to go back to Canada to untangle all the complications arising from the administration of my bequests. That took several years. And it exacted a toll on my career. The calls and offers from law schools and universities dried up. Ten years of study and professional training went out the window. I was saved by the fact that I had acquired so much business experience and life experience managing three estates that I was able to launch an inheritance consulting business and found a company that creates articles, books and films. In a sense, I became my own law firm and my own university.

Now, you may be thinking, "That's nice, Mike. You came out on the other side, more or less in one piece, and you've got some good advice for other heirs. But I'm not sure I should keep reading this book. It doesn't have much to do with me. I mean, heirs are people like the Rocke- fellers, the Kennedys or the Fords." Well, if you're thinking this, you're wrong. For the first time in North American history, inheritance is becoming a general fact of life. I be- gan to realize this when people from so many different backgrounds came to me for assistance. I was struck by how many people were having experiences similar to mine. This inspired me to do some research. I went to the public library and looked up articles on wealth and inheritance in newspapers, magazines and journals. I found that the press and academics had recently been writing quite a lot about inheritors. My generation, the baby boomers, those 74 million folks born between 1946 and 1964,[1] who are now somewhere between the ages of 33 and 51, had been dubbed "The Inheritance Generation." I had been so busy dealing with my own inheritance that I hadn't seen that my experience, which, at first, I thought was exceptional, was an example of a general trend.

I was stunned to learn that economists Robert Avery and Michael Rendall were reporting that over the next 50 years my generation would inherit around $10 trillion, coming in 115 million bequests, with an average bequest valued at around $90,000.[2] At least 60 percent of younger Americans stand to inherit $49,000 or more. In the last five years alone, 2.4 million bequests, totaling more than $365.7 billion, had already been received.

I was amazed when I saw the figures on bequests that would accrue to the wealthiest 20 percent of American families. They control almost 80 percent of America's wealth, which means that 7.6 million households own over $8 trillion in assets. These assets will be inherited over the next four decades by approximately 15 million younger Americans; an average bequest will be worth about $500,000.[3]

In Canada, I found that the inheritance picture mirrors the American. According to Ralph Hicks and Len Kubas, Canada's leading consultants on wealth concentration among older Canadians, 45 percent of all personal assets are owned by persons 50 years or older. This group represents about 3.2 million Canadians who will pass on an average of $100,000 in assets to each of their children over the next three decades.

These figures have excited some envious commentary by the press. Baby boomers have been accused of being the most spoiled generation on record. For years, they enjoyed privileges provided by parents who profited from the post-war economic boom. College degrees, cars and down payments on homes became commonplace for an entire generation. Now, the press says, boomers will enjoy an inheritance windfall. It's kind of like getting your cake after you've already eaten it.

As I looked around at the lives of my friends and acquaintances, this image of pampered young people didn't always seem to fit the reality. The image of spoiled boomers certainly applied to a small group that attended elite schools, lived in major cities and profited from the financial boom of the 1980s. But my experience and research told me that most young people led different lives during the 1970s and 1980s. While some members of the media tried to convince us that a tiny minority of "Yuppies" represented an entire generation that had lost itself in the selfish pursuit of gain, in fact most young Americans were neither that selfish nor that successful.

As I continued to comb through articles and clippings, I discovered that during the 1970s and 1980s, income growth stalled for most members of the middle class, and this, of course, included boomers who had only recently entered the work force. Experts seemed to agree on a basic fact: Since 1973, the real value of median family income has remained more or less constant at around $30,000. In other words, families whose incomes were halfway between the top and bottom of all income earners in the late 1980s could not buy more things with their income than they could have with a mid-range income in 1973. In a recent book about middle-class misfortunes, *Boiling Point*, Kevin Phillips proved that by the late 1980s and early 1990s, in spite of the rapid growth in some areas of the United States, most young people were not better off. By 1991, the purchasing power of family incomes had fallen back to the levels of the late 1970s.[4]

During this 20-year period, not only did middle-class incomes level off, but the number of people enjoying middle-class lives actually declined. Between the early 1970s and early 1980s, the number of people aged 25 to 55 with middle-class incomes declined from 75 percent of the population to 67 percent.[5] This stagnation in income was also matched by a stagnation in savings and wealth. Phillips reports that in 1991, Americans between the ages of 35 and 44 were only half as wealthy as their parents had been at the same age. Ironically, during the peak years of the Reagan boom (1984 to 1988), the median net worth of all households declined by 4 percent.[6] Based on this trend, economists Frank Levy and Robert Michel predict baby boomers will reach retirement with only half the wealth their parents had when they retired: $143,000 versus $293,000.[7]

The causes of the declining fortunes of younger Americans have been well-documented. During the 1970s and 1980s, they faced a series of economic obstacles that their parents never had to face: diminishing productivity, high inflation, escalating private and public debt, high interest rates, high taxes, a shrinking manufacturing base, foreign competition in key consumer goods, and spiraling increases in the cost of medical care, housing and college tuition. And due to the perilous state of Medicare and Social Security, boomers cannot expect the state to provide them in old age with the same benefits their parents are receiving.

The media image of a greedy, spoiled generation may apply to a privileged few, but not to most baby boomers. For many, especially those in their 30s, even getting close to the financial achievements of their parents will depend on receiving gifts or bequests. The younger generation will need their inheritance windfall if they hope to equal the standard of living they enjoyed as kids.

Unfortunately, many of these heirs will find that preserving and enhancing a bequest is tricky business. In my consulting practice, I discovered that most heirs make financial mistakes. This isn't because they suddenly become playboys and wastrels who blow their fortunes on luxury goods and foolish business schemes. Rarely have I found that immaturity, irresponsibility or frivolity are the main causes of hardship. Heirs tend to have financial problems because the very experience of inheritance is fraught with internal tensions and contradictions that impair personal insight and sound business judgment. In the following chapters, I will explain this point by showing you how the symptoms of grief and what I refer to as the symptoms of affluence can undermine the qualities needed to manage an inheritance successfully.

My method and design are unconventional. I begin with examples of problems with inheritance drawn from my experiences and the experiences of clients and friends and use them to develop some general rules of conduct I hope will be useful in a practical way to any heir. At the same time, I use social science, psychology, psychiatry and great works of literature to help us reflect on the symptoms of grief and affluence and how they can adversely affect the management of an inheritance. My hope is that this approach will yield a richer and more comprehensive account of the oppositions inherent in the experience of inheritance and the lessons we must learn in order to overcome them.

# Chapter 2

# The Dangers of Unresolved Grief

Victor was only 17 years old when his father suffered a fatal heart attack. About to graduate from high school with high grades in science, Victor had dreamed of becoming a doctor and had secured a place in premedical studies at the University of California. But his father's death changed all that. Victor came from a traditional working-class family in which his dad (a construction foreman) had been the breadwinner and his mom stayed at home to raise the kids. As the eldest child and only son, he was left with the responsibility of providing for the family. He had to give up his place in the premed program and go to work as a roofer to support his mom and his three younger sisters, who were all under the age of 10.

Victor never complained about his situation. He quietly followed in the footsteps of his father, a reserved man who had never flinched in the face of adversity. Not once, even during the funeral, did Victor shed a tear. Remarkably, 15 years passed before Victor allowed himself to openly grieve his father's death. After attending a funeral service for an older gentleman, a neighbor with whom he had only a social acquaintance, he began to weep uncontrollably. At first, he couldn't understand why. Later, back at work and still in tears, it suddenly hit him. He had always noticed a slight physical resemblance between the neighbor and his father. He realized he was revisiting his father's death through the funeral of his neighbor and finally shedding the tears he had held in for so many years.

Victor faced a problem common to most bereaved people: He didn't know he hadn't finished grieving. The process of expressing and releasing intense sadness, regret, guilt, or anger lasts longer than we sometimes think—more so when we try to suppress our feelings like Victor did.

Victor's stoicism gave him the strength to make personal sacrifices for the sake of his family, and in that sense it may have been a virtue. However, this virtue can easily become a vice when a survivor has to manage an inheritance. When an inheritor's grief remains unexpressed and unresolved, symptoms can manifest themselves indirectly as errors of judgment in financial and personal matters.

Consider what happens when someone is suffering from depression, a common symptom of grief. Depression manifests itself as an inability to imagine a future that promises happiness or at least some relief from present suffering. When the future is rendered opaque, an inheritor cannot anticipate all the contingencies that an effective financial plan must be prepared to meet. If, for example, depression

prevents an investor in real estate from carefully considering possible swings in interest rates or how changes in
demographics might affect demand, he could end up losing
a lot of money.

Studies conducted by psychologists and psychiatrists
during the last 20 years point to two ways in which bereaved people can mismanage an inheritance. The first is
to make key personal or financial decisions while in the grip
of any of the basic symptoms of grief, such as depression.
The second is to make key decisions while experiencing self-
confusion, which expresses itself as a paralyzing uncertainty
about what to do, what to believe in and what kind of person to be. It is the final or ultimate symptom that results
from experiencing the basic symptoms. In this chapter, I
want to show you that you must become aware of the
symptoms of your grief and how the failure to resolve them
can cause you to mismanage your inheritance.

In what follows, I take you on a tour of the grieving
process and begin by listing the primary symptoms, as
identified by leading therapists, to help you recognize and
track your emotional state.

1. **Numbness**—Numbness is simply the absence of
   an emotional reaction to receiving news of a death.
   It results from denial, that is, the unwillingness to
   recognize and suffer the loss; it protects us tempo-
   rarily from overwhelming emotions, particularly
   when a death is sudden and unexpected.[1]

2. **Shock**—Some therapists refer to shock as numbness or an extreme emotional outburst (i.e., raving,
   screaming).[2] In other words, some identify it as denial of the loss and others as immediate acknowledgment of the loss. While it is often associated

with learning of a sudden death, some therapists have observed it in survivors who lose someone to a lengthy terminal illness.[3]

3. **Disbelief and denial**—These symptoms result from a *temporary* inability to recognize and suffer the loss (i.e., numbness) or a *sustained* inability to recognize and accept the loss.

4. **Anxiety**—Anxiety or worry is linked to two related fears. The first is the general fear of one's own death (a common experience among survivors); the second is the fear of not surviving without the aid and comfort of the deceased.[4]

5. **Restless overactivity**—This results from the nervous system's reaction to bereavement. Obviously, the death of a family member or friend on whom you depended for essential support presents a threat to your welfare, so much so that you might feel your very survival is threatened.[5] In response, your system pumps out adrenaline to give you alertness and energy to meet the dangers ahead. Unfortunately, this energy is rarely put to good use. The resulting overactivity is usually aimless and stifles any ability "to initiate and maintain organized activity."[6]

6. **Sadness**—Sadness could be described as extreme disappointment or despair caused by losing the pleasure and security, or some other form of well-being, which had been provided by the deceased.

7. **Preoccupation with the deceased**—This takes the form of obsessive thinking about the deceased;[7] it can be a form of denial[8] (i.e., an attempt to hold on to the deceased) or part of a review process

whereby the survivor tries to hold on to essential memories of the deceased or deal with ambivalent feelings about the deceased.

8. **Yearning**—This is a sustained longing to be reunited with the deceased;[9] it's really an extreme version of the feeling of missing someone.[10]

9. **Anger**—This is a common and often confusing feeling that can present itself in a number of different ways. It can be directed against yourself from frustration that you didn't prevent the death (but somehow "should have"). It can be directed externally from a need to make sense of the death by blaming it on others.[11] It can also be directed externally as a means of protecting yourself from people who remind you of the reality of your loss.[12] Other explanations are based on highly speculative genetic and psychological theories.[13]

10. **Guilt and self-reproach**—These feelings arise from blaming yourself for failing to treat the deceased better prior to his or her death.[14] They are most evident in cases in which the survivor had a difficult or ambivalent relationship with the deceased and is then deprived by untimely death of the opportunity for reconciliation.[15]

11. **Depression**—Sadness can turn into depression when feelings of disappointment and despair are accompanied by a general loss of self-esteem, a general sense of guilt and extreme hopelessness.

12. **Diminished self-concern**—This symptom is commonly exhibited by anyone who suffers from depression or a preoccupation with the deceased.[16]

In both cases, the diminished self-concern is brought on by a loss of self-esteem.

Survivors will not necessarily experience all these symptoms or experience their symptoms (whatever they may be) in this order, although numbness and shock are usually associated with early reactions to a death. Symptoms may also be greater in intensity or duration depending on the nature and extent of other losses that might result from a death. These so-called "secondary losses"[17] might include a loss of income, status, dreams, aspirations[18] or a loss of support among family members and friends. Obviously, a survivor's grief reaction can also be affected by many other factors such as the circumstances and manner of death, previous experience with loss and cultural or religious beliefs, just to name a few.

In attempting to make grief a coherent experience for their patients, many therapists try to fit these 12 symptoms into a series of stages. Here we see a survivor's reaction located in a set of prefabricated categories that describe what Everyman will experience. This has been a popular approach in the mental health field ever since Dr. Elisabeth Kübler-Ross argued in 1969 in her seminal work, *On Death and Dying*, that among the terminally ill, grieving for one's own death takes place in five distinct stages: denial and isolation, anger, bargaining, depression and acceptance. Gail Sheehy followed suit in 1976 in her best-selling work, *Passages*, in which she tried to summarize human experience in seven chronological stages. Sheehy argued that membership in a particular age group will determine one's fundamental perspectives on life. In the 35-to-45-year-old category, for example, we go through the so-called midlife crisis; realizing we won't live forever, we develop a thirst for novel experiences, new careers or new spouses before time catches up with us.

The *Passages* approach to psychology has become popular for at least two reasons: It appeals to the democratic impulse to see ourselves as a society of equals and it gives people who are confused by a complex emotional crisis a quick way of making sense of their experiences. You might not like this approach for the very same reasons. By appealing to our belief in equality, it obscures the fact that people can experience midlife, aging, death and so on, in a variety of ways. If people with serious emotional dilemmas were as similar as the *Passages* crowd claims, they wouldn't need years of one-on-one therapy to achieve self-understanding and self-reconciliation. A therapist would simply tell a patient who fell into one of the typical categories to read a chapter from a Kübler-Ross or Sheehy book to achieve emotional insight and equilibrium. End of session. (Sheehy herself recently rejected her own approach in her latest work, *New Passages*, which explains how new research has broken down the categories she previously espoused.)

Perhaps the greatest danger in stage-based analysis is that its proponents ask us to believe we can live well only if we live out our lives in stages. The stages then become self-fulfilling prophecies rather than guides to what one's life actually is and can be. The *Passages* approach makes for easy reading and temporary relief from psychic confusion. However, the cost of these advantages may be losing the joy and peace of mind that come from understanding the complexity of one's personal experiences.

At this point, you may be thinking that I'm going to leave you with the 12 symptoms of grief and advise you to experience them as you please—backward, forward, completely, partially. And I'd like to do that. However, that would prevent me from giving you useful advice on the management of your inheritance. As I said before, I decided to review the 12 symptoms of grief to help you identify emotions and attitudes that can impair your powers of judgment in personal and financial matters. This list can help you determine when you should put off making major decisions about an inheritance, but it doesn't help you identify when you've overcome these symptoms and can finally make those important decisions. If I can't help you determine when you've reached that point, obviously this book won't deliver on its promise to help you manage your inheritance effectively.

So, reluctantly, I draw on some therapeutic literature that treats the resolution of grief as a four-stage process. I don't insist, nor do the authors of the literature, that these stages must be experienced in serial order or that they are necessarily associated with a specific set of symptoms. They are simply rough guides that may help you identify when you've finally emerged from intense grief.

**Stage One:** In Stage One, you learn to accept the reality of your loss. In other words, you get beyond symptoms of numbness, shock and denial and realize your loved one has been lost permanently (at least in this life).[19] To recognize this fact, you must fully understand how the death occurred by examining the facts surrounding the loss.[20] You may also have to visit places the deceased frequented to establish that he or she is no longer there.

**Stage Two:** In this stage, you confront and examine all the emotions, ideas and behaviors arising from your grief reaction.[21] You may tend to move between confrontation and avoidance of your symptoms until you reach an equilibrium where you can face your loss without experiencing overwhelming pain.[22]

**Stage Three:** In the third stage, you learn how to live without the support and skills of the deceased. You recognize the need to acquire new skills that allow you to pick up the roles that were previously played by the deceased.[23] If you're a widow, for example, you may need to learn the skills of disciplinarian, breadwinner or social organizer. This can be a difficult stage because you may not initially be aware of how important the deceased was in playing essential roles or meeting fundamental needs.

**Stage Four:** Finally, you learn to put your energy into new activities and relationships to satisfy your social and emotional needs.[24] (In referring to new relationships, I don't mean to suggest that if you've lost your spouse, for example, you must remarry to overcome your grief. New relationships can include friendships or acquaintances of any kind.)

Many therapists agree that every survivor will experience these symptoms and phases in different ways. Although certain symptoms tend to show up in certain stages (numbness, shock, denial in the first),[25] almost any symptom can show up at any stage and consequently the stages may overlap.[26] The "softness" of this analysis is also reflected in two other basic facts relating to symptoms. The first is that survivors do not necessarily experience the same set of symptoms: Some may experience anger, others may not. Some may experience sadness and depression; others only sadness, and so on. This, of course, means the *quality* of grief in every stage will tend to vary for every survivor. The second fact is that survivors vary considerably in the time needed to overcome their grief.[27] This means the *quantity* of grief in every stage will tend to vary for every survivor. In this regard, keep in mind that most people mistakenly believe a normal mourning period is 48 hours to two weeks.[28] In fact, resolving grief can take anywhere from six months to four years.[29] Most people will need at least a year to overcome their major symptoms.[30]

While survivors express their grief in different ways, their symptoms leave them in a similar state of physical and mental exhaustion. This is reflected in an inability to concentrate for long periods, general impairment of memory (including absent-minded behavior)[31] and foggy thinking. These symptoms will eventually express themselves in a sense of general confusion concerning every aspect of a survivor's life.[32] Here we find the second way in which grief can lead someone to mismanage an inheritance—making decisions while experiencing self-confusion.

Therapists believe this confusion has three different causes. The first is the overwhelming stress that grief entails. Losing a loved one who provided you with sympathy, encouragement and advice presents a challenge to your survival; it leaves you insecure and apprehensive about the future. It can also leave you with the overwhelming feeling that you are no longer in control of your life[33] (because you've lost someone who helped you to negotiate obstacles and setbacks). The body responds to this challenge by producing adrenaline.[34] This "survival response" helps you to cope with your loss but it also exacts a toll on your system. You can remain in a state of alarm for only so long. Eventually you begin to feel strain, the body uses up its defensive resources, and you become totally fatigued and confused.[35]

The second cause of this confusion is what therapists call "grief work." It is the process of working through the various stages or phases of grief. Conceiving recovery from grief as "work" is the key to understanding how it can affect judgment. Accepting, experiencing and overcoming the painful feelings and ideas that accompany grief consume mental and emotional energy normally devoted to other pressing matters.

Finally, confusion is caused by the task of learning how to live without someone who played an essential role in your life. This is what we referred to earlier as Stage Three of grief work. Confusion can arise at this stage from the need to play new roles previously played by the deceased. You may have to learn financial skills that had been supplied by your father. You may have to learn to mediate family conflicts in the place of your mother; you may have to play mother *and father* to three young children. You may also become confused as you lose roles you played for the deceased that gave you a sense of purpose and identity.[36] Without your ailing mother, you can no longer play the role of patient care-giver. Without your brother, you lose the role of confidant. Without your husband, you lose *the* person who recognized and nurtured your most important qualities as mother, wife and friend. As you're forced to learn new roles and give up old ones, you might become confused about who you are and what you should do.

Self-confusion can also emerge at this stage because you may not realize immediately all the ways in which the deceased contributed to your welfare. You might make a decision based on your accustomed way of solving problems only to find that it ends in personal or financial disaster. You might become bewildered because the old way of doing things just doesn't work without the advice and insights of your parent or spouse. Best-selling author Lynn Caine, in one of her last books, *Being a Widow*, captures the excruciating problems she faced in making major decisions on her own after losing her husband to cancer:

> *Though I didn't realize it at the time, my life was completely out of control. I had no idea how or where to start putting things back into some kind of order. I felt like the world had exploded, and my job was to find all the pieces and make them fit together again. I was overwhelmed by and unable to cope with the task.*
>
> *There was no one to tell me to stay still, to make no major decisions, to maintain the status quo until I had regained the ability to think clearly again. Instead, I made the classic widow mistake. I uprooted myself and my children and made a disastrous move from the city to the suburbs. In my craziness, I thought that because my life had changed, I had to change my life as well. I thought that by making major decisions I could force my life back together again. I couldn't have been more wrong.*[37]

When you reach this point, you can begin the process of learning new skills that will enable you to survive and prosper without your loved one. This is also the point where you need to find new friends and advisers to take the place of the friend and adviser you've lost.

We might assume that this confusion or disorientation would be severe in the case of someone like Caine, who lost her husband in her 30s and was left to raise two young children on her own, but less so when an adult loses an elderly parent. After all, adults in their 50s expect to lose their parents as they move into their 70s and 80s—don't they? Surprisingly, many therapists believe the reaction can be just as intense, for a number of reasons. The death of an aged parent may lead to the shocking realization that time isn't on your side and you're next in line. It may also produce intense sadness because you've lost that one person who, in witnessing your most important childhood and family experiences, could confirm who you are and where you came from. In this respect, you're grieving for losing a part of yourself. You may also feel intense insecurity or anxiety because you can never again "go home" for comfort and support when things get rough. If you've lost a surviving parent, for the first time you may feel totally abandoned, as if you're an orphan.[38] In this frame of mind, you may also experience intense anger about being left alone to deal with vexing estate problems.

Earlier, I promised to use the four-stage analysis of grief to assist you in determining when you have moved beyond the 12 basic symptoms of grief, to which we can now add self-confusion as the symptom that results from dealing with all the others.

Perhaps the best way to track your progress using this model is to enlist the assistance of a mental health professional—a social worker, psychologist or psychiatrist. This should certainly be done if you have inherited a large or complicated estate that requires full-time management. A therapist can assist you in doing the "work" of grieving in the following ways. He can help you to fully recognize the fact and meaning of your loss by getting you to review and talk about how it happened (Stage One); he can liberate you from intense emotions and ideas by giving you an opportunity to discuss and express them in confidence (Stage Two); he can help you to pinpoint the need to learn and develop new skills and roles to replace those lost with the deceased (Stage Three); and he can help you to overcome the reluctance to move on and pursue new activities and relationships (Stage Four).[39]

Frequently, only a professional can determine when you have emerged from the process of doing "grief work" and are ready to make sound personal and financial decisions. Some of the signs of recovery a therapist can help you to detect are renewed energy, a return to stable eating and sleeping habits, an ability to make better judgments in your daily affairs,[40] the ability to think about the deceased without overwhelming sadness[41] and a sense of release (you are no longer obsessed with memories of the deceased, plagued by loneliness, fixated on the deceased's possessions or compelled to continue activities you shared with the deceased).[42]

Caine believes one of the most helpful ways to promote healing in the later stages of grief is to set a new goal for yourself. This can help you move through the third and fourth stages and learn to live a full life without the presence of your loved one. Caine offers two examples of widows who began to emerge from their grief when one took up flying, an activity her husband had always discouraged, and the other driving, after spending her entire life being chauffeured by her husband:

> *The point is that being involved in setting and achieving a goal is one of the ways you recommit yourself to life. It's a way to create a positive atmosphere in which you can begin to heal. It allows you to feel a certain amount of control over events again. And think about how much freedom the widow who learned to drive gave herself. I don't think I'll ever stop setting goals for myself. It's one of the best habits I've developed.*[43]

So far we've been dealing with so-called "normal" grief reactions. In other words, we've canvassed the symptoms that most grieving people will experience and eventually overcome. Unfortunately, a significant group of grievers (approximately 20 percent)[44] get lost or stuck in some stage of the grieving process and develop long-term emotional or physical problems that often require professional treatment. Long-term unresolved grief presents a special threat to any inheritor. You may, for example, follow my advice and wait a year or more before making important decisions about your bequest and then make a move that ends in deep personal regret or financial ruin six months later. If you find yourself in that position, you may be suffering from a lingering form of grief that has clouded your horizon for so long you no longer recognize the damaging effect it's having on your outlook. Here are the major forms of pathological grief you might experience:

1. **Absent grief**—As the term implies, you enter into deep denial. You simply refuse to acknowledge that a loss has occurred.[45] Grieving becomes a longer-term experience since the acknowledgment of loss, which sets grieving in motion, occurs at a much later point.

2. **Delayed grief**—A survivor will recognize that a loss has occurred and experience some symptoms of grief while others go underground and express themselves later (even years later). During the delay period, other symptoms indicating the presence of repressed grief may develop, such as overactivity without a sense of loss, replication of the symptoms of the last illness of the deceased, psychosomatic conditions (such as ulcerative colitis, rheumatoid arthritis and asthma) or self-isolation.[46]

A reaction can be delayed when you have pressing responsibilities that prevent you from working through all your symptoms.[47] Survivors who have demanding professional lives or are left with the duty of maintaining family morale or providing for family members[48] are the most likely candidates for this problem. Latent symptoms will often be triggered by a subsequent death or loss of some other kind (for example, a job loss, the death of a pet) or even by a film or play that portrays a loss similar to the one you've experienced.[49] The sign that latent symptoms are emerging is that your reaction to the subsequent loss is wildly exaggerated and out of proportion to its actual impact on your life[50] (as was the case with Victor, whose story opened this chapter).

3. **Chronic grief**—Identified as the most common syndrome, chronic grief is present when painful symptoms last for an unbearably long time.[51] This often occurs when a survivor loses someone on whom he or she was extremely dependent;[52] widows and widowers are prime candidates in this category. Early signs that a survivor may be moving toward a chronic reaction are low self-confidence (about managing alone) and extreme insecurity, as well as intense pining and feelings of helplessness. A dependent survivor holds on to grief to avoid moving on and facing the task of living in a new world that has become threatening without the protection and comfort provided by a partner. Specific reactions of the survivor can include withdrawing from life by hiding out at home (extreme pining),[53] nursing a fantasy of a

continued relationship with the deceased by, for example, preparing meals for two every day (denial) or currying sympathy from others who provide substitute forms of support. When any of these symptoms go on and on, you know you're living with a chronic reaction. Chronic grief can also stem from guilt about failing to reconcile with someone with whom you had an ambivalent or difficult relationship. You may feel compelled to grieve endlessly to punish yourself for what you should have said or done.[54]

4. **Unanticipated grief**—This type of grief results from a loss that is sudden and unexpected. Since survivors often find it hard to assimilate such a loss, they often get stuck in the early stages of grief with symptoms such as disbelief, denial and extreme anxiety. (Social withdrawal, depression and self-reproach have also been reported.) These symptoms can become chronic and stay with survivors for up to four years after the loss.[55]

5. **Exaggerated grief**—Also identified as a common syndrome,[56] exaggerated grief is present when one or a few of the symptoms of normal grief become overwhelmingly intense and painful.[57] While absent, delayed, chronic and unanticipated grief are distinguished by the *duration* of their impact on the psyche, exaggerated grief is distinguished by the *intensity* of its impact. The most common distorted symptoms are extreme guilt, self-reproach, anger[58] and depression,[59] which result generally from ambivalent feelings about the deceased. These symptoms can be directed against yourself

or others. For example, when guilt about your omissions is directed with full force at yourself, you may feel depressed and exhibit self-punitive behavior. When the same guilt is directed away from yourself, you may try to saddle others (such as attending physicians, friends or family members) with angry accusations of neglect.[60] Dr. Erich Lindemann first documented these reactions in 1944 in his landmark study of bereavements resulting from a fire at the Coconut Grove, a club in which 450 people celebrating the end of a college football game were killed. His analysis of guilt reactions of bereaved families and those who managed to escape from the club illustrates how guilt can lead someone to make disastrous financial decisions. Lindemann observed that:

> *...most of...[the patient's]...activities attain a coloring detrimental to his own social and economic existence. Such patients, with uncalled-for generosity, give away their belongings, are easily lured into foolish economic dealings, lose their friends and professional standing by a series of "stupid acts," and find themselves finally without family, friends, social status, or money. This protracted self-punitive behavior seems to occur without any awareness of excessive feelings of guilt.[61]*

Exaggerated guilt reactions present perhaps the greatest danger to anyone trying to manage an inheritance.

6. **Anticipatory grief**—The success of medicine in prolonging the lives of the terminally ill has led to an increasing incidence of friends and family members exhibiting the symptoms of grief before the actual loss. Grieving before the fact is a "normal" reaction[62] in anyone who is close to a terminally ill person, yet it belongs in the category of pathological grief because it so often leads to chronic and exaggerated symptoms. It tends to manifest as severe guilt or self-blame, which can translate to severe depression, precisely because you felt and acted as though the loss had already occurred while your loved one was still alive. These symptoms most often arise in the following three situations: accepting the loss at an early point, which leads to later self-accusations of abandoning your loved one when you were most needed;[63] taking over roles previously played by your loved one, such as managing family finances, especially when he or she relinquishes these roles reluctantly; and in the case of inheritors, contemplating the financial rewards that will result from the death of a loved one. Anticipatory grief can also take the form of extreme and prolonged anger if you had to make personal, financial or professional sacrifices to take care of your loved one for an extended period.

\* \* \*

So ends our brief tour of modern perspectives on grief. We can now see that we should avoid making important decisions about an inheritance, in the first instance, when caught in the grip of any one of the 12 extreme feelings or ideas that are at the core of a grief reaction, especially if they have a pathological bent. While it's often said that strong emotions, such as fear, can concentrate the mind, more often than not they impair our ability to perceive and protect our real interests.[64]

If, for example, you are experiencing denial, you may try to obliterate the physical reminders of your loss by selling all the possessions of the deceased.[65] When you finally acknowledge and suffer the loss, you may deeply regret the decision to sell possessions that would have served as comforting mementos. In the grip of intense anxiety, you may be vulnerable to the dishonest broker who plays on fear. When he suggests that you must trade stock if you hope to preserve the value of your portfolio, you might end up shortchanged. If you're angry with a workaholic father who was never home when you really needed him, you might try to punish him, consciously or unconsciously, by squandering your share of his estate. Experiencing guilt about failings in your relationship with your late mother, you might feel you don't deserve your inheritance and waste it on others.

In a state of depression, without optimism or a clear vision of the future, you can easily make unrealistic financial plans that end in disaster. Without sober self-concern, you might make reckless investments that lead to financial ruin.

You can also see that you should defer making major decisions about an inheritance while lost in the self-confusion that results from experiencing and working through the symptoms of grief and learning how to live without someone who was a key role player or role receiver in your life.[66] As you experience shifting perspectives, you might miss key management opportunities or see them when they don't really exist. As you experiment with new versions of yourself, you could make a key financial decision based on one version only to find that it doesn't suit a succeeding one.

This is what happened to Lynn Caine. In her confusion about how to play the new roles of single parent and breadwinner, she mistakenly committed a major part of her inheritance to purchasing a home in the suburbs. When she came to her senses, she realized that in spite of the drastic changes she had endured, she could find happiness only in Manhattan. This turned out to be an expensive lesson for Caine, emotionally and financially, one that would have cost less had someone been there to tell her to slow down and put off making major decisions until she had both feet on the ground.

Chapter 3

# The Syndromes of Grief

A survivor is often advised to speed up the pace of his or her life. Well-meaning friends and not-so-well-meaning employers may encourage you to deal with grief by throwing yourself into your work. "Keep busy and don't think too much and soon you'll be feeling better." If only that were true. Taking that advice to heart only defers the heartache to another day. What you really need to do is simplify and slow down your life so you have the time and energy to endure the pain of grief.[1] If you don't, your grief might remain unresolved, go underground and express itself in errors and oversights that might cause you to lose your job or mismanage your inheritance. In this chapter, I present five case studies describing attitudes that, in my experience, often cause these problems. I refer to these attitudes as the *syndromes of grief.*

A syndrome is simply the combination of two or more harmful symptoms of any physical or psychological ailment.

Applied to the following case studies, a syndrome is defined as the presence of two symptoms that can cause financial ruin: a symptom of grief (denial, anxiety, anger or guilt) and its secondary manifestation (imprudence, foolishness or recklessness in dealing with financial, professional or personal matters).

# 1. The Syndrome of Self-Sufficiency

One of the common causes of mismanaging an inheritance is the belief that you can handle all aspects of your wealth on your own. Refusing to seek out the opinions of friends and experts, sooner or later, you make a foolish financial move that precipitates a significant loss. This self-imposed isolation usually results from denial. To avoid facing the sorrow and other difficulties caused by bereavement, you create a myth of god-like self-sufficiency. Helen Barnes's mismanagement of her family's trucking business illustrates this problem.

In 1970, Ben Barnes had founded a small but successful regional trucking business in Toledo, Ohio, which delivered auto parts from local suppliers to in-state assembly plants. When Barnes died in 1985, his wife, Henrietta, took over the business and, surprisingly, increased the company's market share even though previously she had never participated directly in the company's affairs. Her success was based on two sterling business qualities. She had a keen eye for the bottom line, an attribute honed during 20 years as a bank employee; she also turned out be a shrewd judge of character, a trait that made her a savvy dealer and a good manager of personnel. Initially skeptical of her abilities, the firm's rough-and-tumble truckers soon referred to her with respect and affection as "Mother Hen."

Sadly, the stress of running this 24-hour-a-day business in a very competitive field took its toll on Mrs. Barnes. After five years as president, she died on the job, the victim of a stroke at the age of 63. She left three heirs: one son, Tom, 27, an apprentice in the business who handled truck maintenance, and two daughters, Susan, 30, a homemaker with two small children, and Helen, 37, a chartered accountant with a solo practice.

Helen, who was named executor, faced the formidable task of maintaining her practice while administering all the estate assets, including the trucking business, which she desperately wanted to keep in the family. During the first six months of her executorship, Helen held it all together by working seven days a week, from nine in the morning to eleven in the evening. Then exhaustion caught up with her. She became ill and was unable to recover until she reduced her workload by ceding some managerial authority to Tom.

Unfortunately, once clothed with executive status, Tom became quite ambitious and attempted to usurp the authority of the logistics officer and personnel manager, Ralph MacAuley, who had been with the firm for close to 20 years. No one knew the business better than Ralph, who had been the key figure assisting Henrietta in taking over management of the firm after her husband's death. Feeling that he was going to be replaced by Tom, Ralph took early retirement, a move that soon highlighted the inadequacies of Helen's management style.

Shortly after Ralph's departure, Helen faced two business crises. First, she made an error on a corporate client's income tax return, which led to a claim by Internal Revenue against the client for $100,000 in additional taxes and a $15,000 late payment penalty. The client satisfied the claim and then launched a negligence suit against Helen. The second crisis was created by a competing trucking firm that sensed instability at Barnes and decided to test its competitive mettle by offering cut rates to Barnes's preferred customers.

Helen was so busy trying to hold on to her own clients that she hadn't seen the rate war coming. Tom hadn't seen war on the horizon either. He was well-liked in the firm and had an excellent knowledge of truck maintenance but he turned out to have poor business judgment. To make matters worse, recently Helen had allowed Tom to make an investment in new refrigerated trailers to develop business in the farm produce market. Ralph's insight and experience were sorely missed.

Helen had the good sense to cut the shipping rates in lock step with her competitor. This allowed Barnes to hold on to most of its existing clients in the auto sector. Yet, having invested its cash reserves in refrigerated trailers, the firm didn't have the resources to deal with a reduced revenue stream. Eventually, Barnes had to borrow heavily against its assets to meet its cash shortfalls. Six months later, having failed to make serious inroads in the farm market and deeply in debt, the company went belly up.

Ralph had foreseen the demise of the company. That's one of the reasons he took early retirement. He knew that Helen couldn't run two complex businesses on her own. Why hadn't Helen recognized this obvious fact at an earlier point?

Helen had at least three alternatives for dealing with her family's inheritance: She could have taken in a partner at the accounting office to lighten her workload and free up the time needed to oversee the trucking firm and find a new manager for it. She could have given up her accounting practice to manage the trucking firm full-time. Or she could have kept her practice and sold the business. Obviously, each solution would have exacted a serious cost (i.e., losing control of her practice, losing her practice outright or losing Barnes Trucking). That is the clue to understanding why she failed to choose any of these rational alternatives and took the irrational route of running two businesses at once.

Helen had been very close to her mother and, in fact, was dependent on her for both companionship and support. A lonely careerist who, unlike her younger siblings, had never married, Helen was a frequent visitor at her mother's home at dinner time and on weekends. Of the three children, she was most devastated by her mother's death and did everything she could to avoid facing the pain of her loss. Helen's need for denial was so strong that she couldn't begin to face the secondary losses, such as the sale of Barnes Trucking or her career, that would have accompanied realistic plans for dealing with her mother's estate. As a result, she couldn't resolve the tension between her commitment to her career and her commitment to the family business. Helen sought refuge from pain and reflection in the opiate of endless work. When she finally woke up, all was lost.

## 2. The Syndrome of Dependency

Another way that heirs often court financial ruin is to leave the management of their wealth completely in the hands of the experts. This syndrome can reflect a need for the denial of pain, as well as the avoidance of guilt or anger. If you have trouble facing the emotional consequences of losing a loved one, you may be unwilling to face the financial consequences as well. Thus, you carry on with your life as though nothing momentous had happened and leave the management of your inheritance to others. This leaves you vulnerable to manipulation, negligence and fraud. Such was the fate of Leo Feldman.

Leo was a 23-year-old musician trying to launch a career as a singer and songwriter when his father, a prominent physician in Palo Alto, was killed in a car accident. Dr. Feldman left Leo $350,000 in cash, which he placed with professionals who squandered almost the entire amount. To understand how and why this happened, we need to acknowledge that Leo and his father had never gotten along very well.

Dr. Feldman had been a very busy fellow. In addition to being a well-known specialist in the field of oncology, he had been a highly successful investor in the stock market and a tenured professor at Stanford's medical school. Leo had always resented the fact that his father had been so busy meeting with patients, students and brokers that he rarely had time to spend with his family. Leo had never seen his dad as a role model, an attitude that had been hardened by Dr. Feldman's grating insistence that his son follow in his footsteps and find a professional calling. He had implored Leo to pull up his grades so he could gain admission to a highly ranked college that would give him the profile to compete for a place in law or business school. Leo, however, never took much interest in academic or financial achievement.

At any rate, Leo got his talents from his mother's side of the family, which included a long line of artists, musicians and designers. From an early age, he had studied music privately and, by the time he was a teenager, was writing his own songs and playing in several high school bands. Against his father's wishes, he decided to skip college to form a band, which he took on a year-long tour of the southwestern states. The tour gave him the exposure he needed to land a five-year management deal with a well-known agent, Barney Blume.

With this deal in hand, Leo felt he was on the verge of proving to his father that giving up college to pursue his love of music wasn't a mistake. But, at that very moment, Dr. Feldman was killed.

Dr. Feldman left the bulk of his estate, close to $2 million, to his wife, and $100,000 in trust to each of his teenage daughters to pay for their college educations. Leo was astonished when he received a lawyer's letter informing him that he would receive more than three times his sisters' shares—$350,000 in cash—with no strings attached. How could his dad have trusted him with that much money?

Dr. Feldman left no instructions in his will concerning Leo's bequest, and that was by design. Secretly he had hoped that leaving a considerable sum in Leo's hands would force him to acquire the experience and stature of a successful professional. In fact, quite the opposite happened.

Leo decided not to deal with his inheritance. He turned over the management of the bequest to his agent, Blume, and Blume's lawyer, accountant and broker. He told himself that this was the wisest course for a couple of reasons. First, his experience in the music business had taught him that financial matters were always better handled by other parties; delegation freed an artist to concentrate on creating good music. Second, he had observed that his father had always relied on a wide range of other professionals in his own business dealings.

It didn't take long for Blume and his lawyer to hatch a business scheme to start Leo's own recording company (he had yet to sign a record deal); it was sold to Leo as a way to quickly launch his career. The cost of startup was $200,000. They placed the remaining $150,000 with the broker, who promised to treat the account as Leo's nest egg and invest it in a safe mix of stocks and mutual funds.

A year later, Leo began bouncing rent and utility checks. When he pressed Barney to explain where the money went, he received vague, unsettling assurances, such as, "Don't worry, kid, this business has its ups and downs; things will change soon enough." When he approached his lawyer, he was told to talk to his broker. But whenever he called his broker, whom he had met only once, the day he handed over the check for $100,000, he couldn't get a return call. Finally, at the urging of a friend, he hired an accountant experienced in the entertainment field to investigate the entire situation. Here's what Leo learned about his affairs:

Leo's first discovery was that Barney had set up the record company to serve his own financial interests, not Leo's. Barney had used the label to build his own stable of artists, spending most of the original $200,000 investment to sign other acts. And when the new groups failed to turn out any hit songs, the company quickly went into the red. Barney had also shortchanged Leo by signing a one-sided distribution deal for his new CD. Although the CD had sold well in California (20,000 copies in year one), Leo hadn't received much of a return because most of the revenue went to Barney and the distributor until sales hit 25,000 units. As for Leo's broker, he spent all his time tending to the affairs of his wealthier clients, having taken Leo's relatively small account as a favor to Barney. As a result, Leo was stuck with a bundle of declining stocks that had never been managed properly. Finally, a lot of money had been spent on professional fees. Since Leo hadn't monitored his experts, they had met and called one another frequently without regard to cost. This led to outrageous billings. A year and a half after receiving his certified check for $350,000, Leo's company was on the verge of bankruptcy and his portfolio had dwindled to $80,000.

As Leo surveyed the wreckage, he slowly realized that he had been fooling himself about his motives for placing his bequest in the hands of Barney and his cohorts. True, he needed to devote his time to getting out his own work, but he wasn't a star overwhelmed by the demands of constant touring. He certainly had enough spare time to keep an eye on his finances. And his father's habit of using several different professionals in his business dealings? Well, he had conveniently blocked out that his father had carefully studied every professional opinion he ever received and had often used his experts to comment on the viability of one another's advice. Why hadn't he seen that his schedule and his father's example pointed toward hands-on management rather than a complete delegation of authority?

On reflection, Leo had to admit that his stormy relationship with his father had colored his judgment. In losing his father so suddenly, he had been deprived of the opportunity for reconciliation. This, he realized, had left him with regret and guilt about all the harsh words that had passed between them over the years. He also recognized that he was harboring guilt about feeling relieved that his father had died; he had experienced a strange liberation in never again having to endure his father looking down on his alternative lifestyle. Because he had been reluctant to face the emotional legacy of his father's death, Leo had trouble facing the financial legacy as well. Placing the demands of his inheritance on others had been part and parcel of an unconscious strategy of avoiding his guilt. When

Leo fully understood all this, he became very depressed and found a new reason to feel guilty: How he could ever forgive himself for losing so much of his father's hard-earned fortune?

Leo learned to play it safe and stay on top of his own finances. He sold off his portfolio and placed the proceeds (around $75,000) in a savings account where they remained as security against the vicissitudes of his music career. Several years passed, however, before he came to terms with the complex guilt arising from his father's death. And, paradoxically, the losses themselves were the key to overcoming it. He eventually learned to respect his father's business acumen and think of it as something worth emulating. Losing $275,000 was the price he paid to gain peace of mind.

# 3. The Opportunity Syndrome

Anxiety is perhaps the most common attribute of grief among those who lose a spouse or family member. It stems from a legitimate concern about how one will cope without the support and comfort of the deceased. This worry makes survivors extremely vulnerable to hucksters and deal makers when they pitch products and investments. After all, every financial pitch is an implicit appeal to fear. When, for example, a stockbroker tells you, "This deal may never come along again," he's really saying, "Invest now or your financial future will never be secure." When an insurance company advertises its policies and annuities, it sends a similar message: "Fear the uncertain future; invest now, or you and your family will end up in the poorhouse." Fearing the future as they do, survivors are often taken in by these pitches and end up making investments that waste their inherited wealth. This is what happened to

Jake Dupont, a 45-year-old school teacher from Wisconsin, after both his parents died in the same year.

During the previous two-year period, Jake's parents had been in and out of hospitals and otherwise cared for at home by nurses and homemakers. Even though they had carried private health insurance, the extended hospital and private care took a huge bite out of their combined estates. After paying off almost $150,000 in medical bills, Jake, who was the executor and sole beneficiary, was left with $100,000 in short-term bonds and Treasury bills. In the wake of these personal and financial losses, Jake became overwrought about the prospect of further loss of any kind. His worst fear became losing his inheritance, which he wanted to set aside for his retirement.

Jake's anxiety made him the perfect target for a local mortgage broker, Ron Baxter. Ron convinced Jake that he had to reinvest his entire inheritance because his after-tax income from bonds and T-bills would never allow him to keep pace with the rate of inflation. He also warned Jake off the stock market as an alternative, arguing that it was too risky for Jake's goal of long-term security. Ron presented a mortgage as the perfect investment vehicle. It would provide him with a high rate of return, anywhere from 10 to 15 percent, and security in property that was destined to increase in value.

Ron offered Jake a "superb deal" on a local 100-acre farm property valued at $300,000. The owner had already given a first mortgage to a bank in the amount of $175,000 with a seven-year term at an interest rate of 10 percent. To finance a shift in usage from corn to soybeans and the acquisition of new farm equipment, the owner wanted to take on a second mortgage for $100,000, which Ron had offered to finance at 14 percent for a three-year term, with principal payable at the end of the term. To assuage any fears Jake had about the stability of the investment, Ron persuaded the owner, who also ran a small insurance business, to offer a personal guarantee for the full amount of the second mortgage, as well as a pledge of several pieces of farm machinery. He also assured Jake that the owner's remaining equity in the property ($25,000) would protect him against default and an exercise of power of sale by Jake or the bank. It would certainly be enough to cover back payments, a real estate commission and lawyers' fees.

Jake took the second mortgage and, a year later, saw the mortgagor go into default after his insurance company, the revenue from which had been used to meet interest payments, went bankrupt. The bank instituted power of sale proceedings and had the property on the market within two months of the default. However, it took almost eight months for the property to sell, and it had to be let go for $235,000. After the bank was paid back and all other expenses were paid out, Jake was left with around $53,000, just a little more than half his original investment. Here's a simple accounting of the loss:

| | |
|---|---:|
| Sale price | $235,000 |
| Principal amount of the first mortgage | − $175,000 |
| Back interest on the first mortgage | − $11,666 |
| Back interest on the second mortgage | − $9,333 |
| Legal fees | − $5,000 |
| Back taxes and utilities | − $6,432 |
| Subtotal | $27,569 |
| Proceeds from sale of farm machinery | + $25,320 |
| **Total** | **$52,889** |

Jake would have been protected if he had actually had a reasonable equity cushion to fall back on. The total loan-to-value ratio of 92 percent was far too high to secure him against contingencies. That left him with a meager cushion of $25,000. A more sensible ratio would have been 70 percent, which would have left him with a cushion of $90,000. In other words, he should have been willing to loan $50,000 on top of the bank's $175,000, but not another $50,000 on top of that. Before committing to the deal, he also should have asked for tax statements from the insurance business to check its viability as a source of interest payments.

Jake didn't take the time to learn how to properly evaluate a mortgage deal because he was so anxious to use his inheritance as a hedge against the future that he left circumspection behind. As a result, his worst fear was realized.

\* \* \*

While anxiety usually points in the direction of reckless activity, it sometimes points in the direction of reckless passivity. This is exemplified by Rita Marsuka, a recently widowed 52-year-old homemaker, who inherited over-leveraged business assets that required some daring to preserve. Rita, however, found herself unable to muster the courage to do what was necessary.

Rita's husband, Dan, had been a successful entrepreneur who had acquired profitable real estate holdings, beginning 20 years earlier with the purchase and development of a resort property on the Florida Panhandle. Using the resort as his base, he later acquired a magnificent residential property and several small apartment complexes in the Fort Lauderdale area. Sadly, four years before his death, Dan had mortgaged the resort to a local bank to generate cash for a new business venture that had failed. The loss so reduced his cash flow from the resort, most of which went to pay interest on the mortgage, that he couldn't upgrade or renovate the premises, which had fallen behind the times in both style and amenities.

By the time of his death, revenue was seriously in decline due to competition from newly constructed hotels in the area. When Rita took over the property, it was on the verge of going into receivership, while family savings were being eaten up by her own living expenses and expenses incurred in putting her son and daughter through private colleges. A further worry was that Dan and Rita had given personal guarantees to the bank, which meant Rita might be forced to liquidate other assets if the sale of the resort didn't cover the loan.

Rita faced two alternatives to foreclosure and a possible run on her other properties by the bank. First, she could sell the apartment complexes to pay down a major portion of the bank debt and reduce monthly payments to a manageable level. Then she could use the remainder to renovate the resort to regain its lost share of the tourist trade and hopefully generate sufficient revenue to meet personal expenses. Second, she could sell the family home, a move that would allow her to pay down a smaller portion of the bank debt and then use the revenue from the apartment complexes to cover personal expenses and bring the bank debt down to a reasonable level. In the interim, she would have to hope that the resort could still attract enough business to finance renovations.

Either alternative looked pretty good. By sticking with the status quo while the bank debt ballooned, she was almost assured of being forced to sell one of her other assets to meet the bank's expected short fall on the sale of the resort. Furthermore, the resort property was ideally situated for future residential development. So sacrificing other properties to hold on to it was really the only practical solution. In a few years, she could sell the resort property for a significant sum that would wipe out the bank debt and probably make back all the money her husband had lost.

Nonetheless, Rita lingered over the alternatives while her lawyer and her children urged her to do something. Finally, the bank foreclosed. She lost the resort and was forced to sell her home to meet the anticipated shortfall. She moved into one of the apartment buildings and managed to live comfortably on the revenue from the complexes but she would never again attain the standard of living she had enjoyed during most of her married life.

How do we explain Rita's irrational aversion to sensible financial risk? Having lost her husband less than a year before, Rita was in no shape to make important financial decisions. She was still so traumatized by her husband's loss that she couldn't face the prospect of also losing the family's assets, even though any hope of securing her family's financial future depended on parting with at least one of them. The result was that she courted the greatest possible risk—foreclosure—and paid a heavy price for it.

## 4. The Don Quixote Syndrome

The romantic heir who wastes his bequest on fantastic business schemes or radical causes doesn't get much sympathy. It's easy to write him off as vain, greedy, immature or just plain stupid. However, in my experience, these qualities, though sometimes present, are usually not the root cause of madcap investing. Many of the heirs who roll the dice and lose are using the euphoria of sudden wealth as a narcotic to deny or avoid the pain of grief. They use an inheritance to lose themselves in an illusory vision that prevents them from experiencing anger, regret, guilt or anxiety. This may very well have been the syndrome that led Huntington Hartford, the real-life heir to the A & P fortune, to waste the better part of his inheritance in a series of improvident ventures. Here I depart from quasi-fictional case studies and recount the actual facts of Hartford's business disasters as chronicled by Lisa Gubernick of *Forbes* magazine.[2]

In 1957, when he was in his 40s, Hartford inherited $90 million of A & P stock, which, adjusted for inflation, would have been worth well over $400 million in 1997. However, after a little more than a decade of bad investing, he was left with approximately $8 million. How could it have happened?

Against the advice of his attorneys who recommended the creation of a diversified stock portfolio, Hartford used his resources to fund a series of visionary experiments in the arts, which eventually cost him millions of dollars.

His first venture was the creation of the Huntington Hartford Foundation, a 154-acre, $600,000 retreat in the Pacific Palisades, which provided free room and board and a stipend for artists who wanted to work for a return to "realism" in the arts. While this may have been a worthy goal, it was out of sync with the times and the foundation folded in 1965. His next costly venture was an attempt to improve the sensibilities of Hollywood. Hartford purchased a large Hollywood Boulevard theater, which he refurbished at a cost of $1 million, with the aim of getting the locals to appreciate classical theater. The locals passed. The theater never turned a profit and after a few years, Hartford was forced to sell it.

Another costly venture was an attempt to found a new magazine of the arts reminiscent of the old *Vanity Fair*, which had gone under during the 1930s. *Show* magazine was a bold attempt to combine aspects of high and low culture—it contained articles by leading intellectuals and erotic photos of beautiful women. While this unusual combination may have been pleasing to Hartford, the public didn't find it appealing. After losing $8 million on the magazine, Hartford wound it up in the early 1960s.

These extravagant ventures set the stage for a final act that cost Hartford almost everything he owned. Hartford and his cousin were sailing off the coast of Nassau in 1959 when they decided to go ashore at Hog Island, a lush 700-acre undeveloped property. Hartford was so smitten with the island that he signed a contract to buy it for $11 million the very same day, without the benefit of independent advice. Renaming the spot Paradise Island, he had a vision of developing a resort that would be distinguished by its architecture, its beautiful women and its "smart talk." In pursuit of his dream, he spent $19 million to build an elite golf course, stables and a Spanish cloister, which was shipped from Spain piece by piece and reconstructed on the island as a 52-room hotel.

Then he faced practical problems that threatened to undermine the entire venture. After making this stupendous investment, he learned that the hotel could become viable only if he built a gambling casino and a bridge connecting the island to the mainland. To do either, he would have to obtain permission from Sir Stanford Sands, the Bahamian minister of tourism and finance. Sir Stanford agreed to grant the necessary licenses if Hartford took on a partner. That man turned out to be James Crosby, a New York business executive, who agreed to co-venture in return for a $2-million loan from Hartford, secured with stock in a private company.

By this time, Hartford was short of cash. The stock he was given couldn't be traded publicly and no private buyer was in sight, so Hartford had to rely on Crosby to find a means of keeping the project solvent. Crosby arranged for a friend, the chairman of the Bank of Commerce of New York, to make a $1-million loan to Hartford, who had to put up most of his remaining share of the island as collateral. The note was payable on demand and guaranteed by Resorts International, Crosby's new company.

Soon thereafter Resorts pulled its guarantee, allowing the bank to call the loan. Since Hartford couldn't make payment, he lost the island. Resorts then paid $13,000 per acre for the property, which eventually became a highly profitable vacation spot. In the end, Hartford netted $2 million from a $30-million investment.

Gubernick concludes that Hartford's demise was ultimately caused by foolishness rather than reckless or careless dealing:

> *Eighty million dollars gone. It's easy to conjure images of Rabelaisian excess, women with weighty baubles, greenbacks piled on a poker table. But they are the wrong illustrations for this tale.... Hartford lost his money because he had aspirations but no business sense.*

Hartford himself pleads ignorance and bad habits that he developed in his youth when he began receiving a considerable stipend from his family: "I was in my 20s, and I had $1.5 million in income a year—all the money I needed.

I never thought about how I would get a return on my investments."

Can Huntington Hartford's quixotisms be blamed simply on a lifelong ignorance of the fundamentals of investing? Can we believe that a graduate of Harvard was unable to learn from early mistakes and develop some business sense? His story could reflect the need to deny the pain of grief. But does it? Perhaps Huntington Hartford was simply a self-indulgent aesthete and playboy who got what he deserved. Whatever the case, his example is worth keeping in mind when you're tempted to blow your inheritance on a yacht, a hand-built sports car or a business venture that promises to quadruple your investment. The big-time spender within you might very well be a fictional character seeking refuge from the symptoms of grief. When you get that urge to spend, consider talking to a good friend or a therapist about your loss rather than talking to a broker or a venture capitalist about your design to conquer Wall Street.

\* \* \*

As you reflect on these syndromes, keep in mind that you can suffer from more than one syndrome at a time. Also be sensitive to the possibility that a particular syndrome could be caused by more than one symptom. Hartford's losses, for example, could have resulted from a need to punish himself for feeling guilty about some unresolved difficulty with his parents rather than a general need to deny the pain of grief. These caveats also apply to our next case studies, which chronicle what I refer to as the *syndromes of affluence*. In these cases, the mishandling of an inheritance results from a transient reaction to dealing with wealth rather than a transient reaction to dealing with grief.

# Chapter 4

# The Syndromes of Affluence

Managing an inheritance can be a huge headache. If you are named the executor of an estate, you'll have to become acquainted with complicated legal and accounting principles and the minutiae of probate procedures. If you are left a fixed asset, such as a home, in another jurisdiction, you may have to move there for a while to guarantee its security and arrange for its sale. If you receive personal possessions, you'll be faced with the tasks of cataloging, evaluating, selling and, in some cases, storing items ranging from furniture and dishes to jewelry and furs. You might also face the unpleasant task of sorting through the clothing and personal papers of the deceased, making agonizing decisions about what should be kept and what should be thrown away. You can be sure that your bequest will present a broad range of emotional and mental challenges.

One of the most important challenges is to avoid pathological attitudes that can develop as a reaction to receiving an inheritance. I refer to these attitudes as the syndromes of affluence. Unlike a syndrome of grief, which, as we saw, is a self-destructive attitude caused by the pain of loss, a syndrome of affluence is a self-destructive attitude caused by the pain of gain. In each of the following case studies, we witness survivors who exhibit symptoms, generated by new-found wealth, that cause each of them to mismanage an inheritance. Each symptom is a reaction to receiving wealth or a reaction to the manner in which a benefactor managed or transferred wealth. Thus, a syndrome of affluence is defined as a symptom of affluence (guilt, anger, vanity, loneliness, jealousy or fear) and its secondary manifestation (imprudence, foolishness or recklessness in dealing with financial, professional or personal matters).

# 1. The "I'm-Not-Worthy" Syndrome

Receiving wealth that you didn't earn can make you feel guilty. This feeling is well described in a paper entitled "The Inheritor's Inner Landscape," published by The Inheritance Project, a group that counsels heirs on charitable giving:

> *Regardless of whether high standards are imposed from within or without, what most heirs eventually discover is that nothing—no martyrdom, no award, no prestigious career—ever completely eliminates the guilt they feel for being handed so much more than others by Lady Luck. For many heirs, then, the fundamental dilemma becomes how to atone for the "crime" they never committed.*[1]

Atoning for this crime can lead to various forms of self-destructive behavior. Perhaps the most extreme example in this regard is Michael J. Brody Jr., grandson of the founder of the business empire built on Good Luck margarine; Brody Jr. flung inherited cash out a window of his Manhattan apartment building and later shot himself in the head.[2]

Guilt is also common when a parent experienced great pain or hardship at the end of his or her life. You might feel that you shouldn't enjoy your inheritance because it was purchased at the price of your parent's suffering. This feeling can lead you to waste your bequest or adopt self-defeating modes of conduct in your professional or private life.

In our next case study, a complicated form of guilt is the principal cause of Vernon Halliday's financial mess.

Vern was a disc jockey for a rock station in Atlanta in the 1970s and early 1980s. He made a decent living, earning around $50,000 a year, working the prime-time evening shift, and picked up another $10,000 to $20,000 by promoting and managing local bands. His life style reflected 1960s idealism; he had an open relationship with his girlfriend, had no kids, liked to party and took vacations in the Third World where he could observe his favorite political movements in action. His one concession to mainstreet America was a small stable of 1960s muscle cars.

Vern was 35 years old when his father, Lamar, who was a successful contractor, died. He left Vern and his brother Dale, an architect in Santa Fe, several rental properties valued at $1.2 million. Dale decided to keep his share of the properties as a retirement investment while Vern cashed in, receiving around $450,000 for his share after taxes and sale-related expenses had been paid. Without giving a second thought to reinvesting the cash, Vern went on a spending binge. He bought a Porsche, threw an all-night party once a week, invested in the bands he worked with and also developed a nasty cocaine habit. By the time his girlfriend got him into a detox program, two years had passed, he had lost his job and blown $350,000.

Working with therapists in the program over a period of months, Vern was able to reflect on how he had lost control of his life. What most surprised him about his behavior was the fact that he had spent his money only on himself and had never given a thought to donating to the political and social causes that he had espoused since he was in his teens. This insight led Vern to a more comprehensive reflection on how he first developed his strong belief in those causes.

As a young man, Vern had battled his father on every important issue, whether it was political or personal. In fact, father and son had been mirror images of each other—stubborn, willful and opinionated. When Lamar wanted Vern to be the first Halliday to attend college, Vern refused to go, even though his father had promised to pay his way. While Lamar had been a decorated World War II veteran who supported the Vietnam War, Vern joined the peace movement and, at one point, worked full-time as a rally organizer. Lamar, whose life reflected strong middle-class values, stressed the importance of paying your dues, avoiding risk, saving as much money as possible, marrying young and raising a family. Vern was a spendthrift who from an early age lived on the fringe, experimenting with alternative life styles.

When Vern moved from grassroots activism to music promotion and radio, his dad was relieved. At least entertainment was a career. And as Vern became a well-known radio personality and began to make more money than his college-educated brother, he gained his father's respect. Lamar would like to have seen Vern married, raising a family and socking away his pennies for a rainy day. But, in the end, he was proud that his son was doing well in his chosen field. Vern was on good terms with his dad when he passed away.

Since Vern wasn't harboring resentments toward his father at the time of his death, he couldn't understand his reckless spending as a need to punish himself for failing to resolve differences with his dad. However, reflecting on his relationship to his father became the key to understanding his actions.

Vern's support of the peace movement, environmental movement and insurgencies in the Third World was, at first, a young man's rebellion against his father's politics. Yet, over the course of two decades, he had held on to those causes as defining aspects of his character. Given their importance in his self-definition, one might have thought that if Vern were to give away his inheritance, he would give it to organizations supporting these causes. In fact, his love of these causes was what led him, in large measure, to waste his inheritance on the pursuit of selfish pleasures. Vern's idealism made him feel guilty about receiving a windfall. Having so long been an enemy of social and economic inequalities, he couldn't really face the fact that he had become a member of a privileged class. When this became clear to Vern in the course of his therapy, he realized that he had been driven to waste his inheritance by an unarticulated guilt that reflected his underlying attitude toward wealth. In recognition of this insight, he celebrated his successful completion of the detox program a year later by making a sizable donation to Greenpeace.

# 2. The "I'm-Too-Worthy" Syndrome

Even though inheritance is a gift, this doesn't prevent heirs from feeling they should have received more. This is often the case when a parent makes unequal bequests to his or her children; unequal shares often leave the less favored feeling angry toward the benefactor and resentful of siblings. The same feelings can arise among children of a first marriage when they lose a major share of their inheritance to the spouse and children of a second marriage. The problem for slighted heirs is that they can't take out their anger on the deceased. Thus, it is often directed against the bequest in the form of reckless investing or against themselves, sometimes in the form of a disastrous career move. The latter is what befell the subject of our next case study, Lon Ellis, a rising star in the world of banking.

Lon's father, David, had been a highly successful stockbroker who had provided his wife, son and daughter with a lavish life style. His success, though, had exacted a high personal toll. The pressure of being a high roller had made David Ellis into a three-pack-a-day smoker and a heavy drinker. These habits caught up with him in 1969 at the age of 55 when he suddenly died of a heart attack.

At the time, David was in the midst of one of his biggest gambles. Anticipating a boom in natural resource production in the 1970s in Latin America, he had invested a major part of his portfolio in extraction industries in Bolivia, Chile, Argentina and Mexico. Unfortunately, political instability and slumping commodity markets didn't cooperate with his gambit. As a result, his family was left with an estate that was heavily in debt. The family's situation was made much worse by the fact that cash reserves that

David had told them would always be on hand for emergencies could not be found in any of his accounts.

Lon and his family went from being millionaires to paupers in a matter of months. David's brother, Vincent, a local attorney who David had named sole executor, was forced to sell the estate's core assets—cars, possessions and the family home—to pay the estate's debts and meet the family's living expenses. However, so little money was left after all debts and expenses had been paid that Lon's mother had to go back to work as a nurse to support the family. Lon and his sister Ashley felt humiliated by their new station and were furious with their father for leaving them so little after providing them with so much during his lifetime. Their ire became rage when they learned from their uncle that some of their father's cash reserves had been spent on other women prior to his death and the rest had been placed in offshore accounts. They were further embittered to learn that the accounts could not be recovered without triggering tax penalties that would wipe them out.

Lon and Ashley responded to their anger by hiding from it. Ashley joined the Peace Corps and was sent to Africa. Lon dropped out of high school just before his senior year, even though he was an excellent student. A year later, he moved to a small town in Washington state where he apprenticed as a carpenter.

After running his own cabinetry business for close to a decade, Lon craved mental stimulation and professional success. He used his savings and proceeds from the sale of his business to finance a B.A. in economics at the University of Washington. After graduating *summa cum laude*, he took a job with a major bank in Seattle and, within five years, rose to become the head of personal banking, a division that served wealthy individuals and family businesses.

Lon was on the fast track to becoming a vice president when $100,000 of client funds went missing in his department. When Lon couldn't immediately explain the loss, the bank launched an investigation that revealed that Lon had been withdrawing client funds from savings accounts and investing them in stocks and debt instruments for his own benefit. Until this recent slip, Lon had always managed to return the principal with interest to the client's account before the end of every month, keeping the difference between the real rate of return and the bank's standard return on savings. As department head, he had deftly employed two strategies to cover up the transactions. He had falsified client authorizations for transfers and deposits and had shifted monies between accounts to cover client demands for cash. Lon was convicted of fraud. Since he had been making a good salary at the bank and had kept most of what he earned from using client funds, he was able to pay back the entire $100,000 loss. As a result, his sentence was reduced to five years of probation and court-supervised therapy.

Lon's activities were puzzling to himself and everyone at the bank. He already had the system working in his favor and was poised for a promotion, a six-figure salary and lucrative stock options. Why had he felt the need to cheat? After six months of therapy, the outlines of the answers were revealed. Lon had dealt with his anger about the injustice of losing most of his inheritance in two indirect ways. First, he had escaped the injustice by becoming a tradesman and joining the back-to-nature crowd in the hinterland, then he tried to make up for it by pursuing a remunerative career in banking.

Both choices had led to more anger. He felt he had wasted his time as a carpenter; he had never made much money and had associated with a group that didn't value his ideas. And, sadly, he never really enjoyed economics or banking and had pursued them only because he thought they would allow him to restore his old way of life. This anger, doubled and redoubled by his efforts to deal with it, had caused Lon to sabotage his life. In the end, he realized that he had taken out his anger for being cheated by cheating others. He had used his clients to help him settle the score; he took their wealth and used it to recover his own. He had been quite clever in rationalizing his behavior—his clients had more money than they needed, he was smart enough to get away with it, nobody got hurt, his bosses didn't realize how much he could have done with more authority. This had helped him to avoid the real reason for his behavior.

With these insights in mind, he re-examined how he had been caught. The oversight that led to the $100,000 loss—a failure to monitor the stock in which he placed the funds on a daily basis—was one he should never had made. He came to believe that he wanted to be caught. His mistake was a way of bailing out of all the unhappiness that his anger had caused him. Still in therapy, Lon's aim is to peel away all the false motivations that his anger inspired and discover what he really wants to do with his life.

## 3. Syndrome of the Vanities

Gratitude for receiving more than you expected can sometimes give rise to a need to make generous donations to charitable causes. The inheritance of grateful heirs brings them a surfeit of joy that allows them to share their wealth with others without diminishing their own pleasure. The giving becomes pathological at a later point when it is motivated solely by a desire to attain a good reputation or exercise dominion over others. This is the point at which generosity, which is good for the donor and the recipient, becomes vain beneficence, which is, at the very least, bad for the donor. The need for recognition can be inexhaustible and has led many a generous heir to give more than he or she could afford. Consider the example of Peter Wingate, a 48-year-old history teacher at Claremont, a private boys' school in Bloomfield Hills, Michigan.

Peter came from old Michigan money that had been handed down on his father's side of the family and, unfortunately, wasted on bad business ventures and high living over the course of the last two generations. One aspect of the remaining wealth was an educational trust fund that had allowed Peter to study history and political science at Columbia College. He was there during the late 1960s when the student movement was reaching its peak, and he had been heavily influenced by its ideology. After graduating, he spent three years in New York working with community groups dedicated to eradicating poverty and improving the public education system in the inner city.

As student activism began to wane in the mid-1970s, Peter moved back to Michigan and took the teaching job. It wasn't long, though, before he found new outlets for his activist bent. He joined a political group in Detroit that was lobbying city and state governments for funds to improve the city's public schools. He also joined an environmental watch group that monitored the pollution control performance of the Big Three automakers. At Claremont, his personal mission was to make his privileged students aware of their "social responsibilities." However, he wasn't very successful in effecting social change there. Colleagues and students resisted his message and accused him of practicing a kind of limousine liberalism. By day, he was a teacher in one of the state's foremost private schools, which drew its patrons from the upper echelons of the auto industry, and yet, by night, he was a virulent critic of the industry's lack of community concern.

One day, quite unexpectedly, he was graced with an opportunity to drive his points home. An uncle on his mother's side of the family, who had a run a small clothing store in Sarasota, died and left a surprisingly large estate valued at close to a half-million dollars. Since he was divorced and did not have children, he left a major share of his estate, $200,000 in bonds and Treasury bills, to his favorite nephew, Peter. Upon learning of his windfall, Peter was overwhelmed. So intense was his gratitude that he wanted to share his good fortune with others who might never have the opportunity to inherit anything. He resolved to donate a hefty sum to a local community group that helped the poor. At the same time, he was attracted to charitable giving by his politics. He thought that an act of charity would allow him to prove to the school that he could put his money where his mouth was, something the money-conscious students would have to respect. He also saw a large donation as a means of making a name for himself in activist circles.

Inspired by these motives, he gave the entire inheritance to a new charity in Detroit that was providing a supplementary head-start program for inner city youth. He couldn't stop bragging about his noble sacrifice, and the hype he got in return was pretty good...for about two weeks. Then, as the talk died down, he realized that his donation wouldn't have a lasting, positive impact on relationships with his students, colleagues and friends. In fact, the opposite occurred. Later that year, when renegotiating his contract, the school administration denied him a raise because, as he later learned from a colleague, the board assumed that anyone who could afford to make such a large donation to a charitable cause didn't need the extra money. His fellow activists also turned on him. His money had introduced a class distinction in their relationship: He was now regarded as a rich guy who couldn't possibly understand their grassroots concerns or appreciate their minimalist life styles.

If all this weren't bad enough, a year later, an audit of the charity revealed that his contribution had been poorly spent. Almost $75,000 had gone to administration, mostly to give raises to key employees, and $50,000 had been spent on new office supplies and miscellaneous overhead expenses. In the end, only $75,000 had been used to provide meals and classes for children in the program.

Peter wished he had kept his ego in check and saved the money for his retirement.

Peter might have satisfied his desire to be generous and his desire for recognition if he had chosen a different financial strategy. If he was hell-bent on donating his entire bequest, he might have used it to start his own foundation to promote the welfare of inner city children. Then he could have guaranteed that the money was spent wisely and also dispensed with the need for approval and cooperation from some of his fellow activists. On the other hand, he might have invested the principal and used the interest income to make smaller yearly contributions to different organizations. This would have given him a continuing profile among activists (one not besmirched by class distinctions) and allowed him an ongoing opportunity to beat his colleagues and students over the head with the message of community concern.

# 4. The Bad-Luck Syndrome

If your inheritance is diminished by some mistake made by your benefactor in managing or transferring his wealth, you might be angered by the injustice of doing with less than you anticipated. As a result, you may become determined to undo the damage. This feeling can lead in two harmful directions. First, it can cause you to pursue the wrong professional or vocational path. Following the example of Lon Ellis (Case Study 2), you might pursue a high-paying career that makes up for the losses but makes you miserable. You might also spend so much time and energy trying to pick up the pieces of a poorly managed estate that you do irreparable damage to your career; you may, for example, lose a promotion or partnership or produce second-rate work that eventually leads to dismissal. Second, your determination can cause you to gamble with the remaining assets to make up for the losses. (Note that a survivor can also experience these reactions if he or she is the one who mismanages the assets and incurs a serious loss.) Variants of these reactions are present in our next case study.

Bill Taylor, a pharmacist and astute businessman, had owned and managed a very successful neighborhood drugstore in Tucson for the last 25 years. For almost two decades, he had been making more than $100,000 a year and had invested the surplus wisely. He had managed to buy the store property, which was now worth $500,000, had amassed a diversified portfolio of stocks worth about $350,000 and, with his wife, Esthelle, shared an annuity plan worth $100,000. (The family home, which had a market value of around $250,000, had been left to them by Esthelle's parents and was owned outright by Esthelle.) As well, he had been able to pay for the college educations of his son Eric and his two daughters Pamela and Vanya.

Now 52 years old, Bill was growing tired of running the business and was looking for a new opportunity. At the same time, he felt that the market dictated a change in business strategy. Several new drugstores, which were part of a large nationwide chain, had recently arrived in Tucson. They were underselling smaller stores in Tucson and, in Bill's case, stealing many of his cost-conscious senior customers. Bill predicted that within five years his pharmacy would be driven out of business. So, a year later, when he was presented with an opportunity to buy a medical clinic, he developed an aggressive business plan to make the venture profitable and secure. While the clinic itself would provide a decent return, the real advantage was the opportunity to build a lab on-site. Currently, clinics in the immediate area were utilizing overbooked labs on the other side of town. By promising to reduce waiting time, Bill thought he could count on a stream of business from local clinics; he could, of course, also count on business from his own clinic. He thought the investment was a sure thing.

To generate capital, Bill sold all his stocks; after capital gains and brokerage fees, he was left with about $320,000. He used every penny to purchase the clinic and build the adjoining lab. A year later, the clinic was doing well; however, the lab was building up a large debt as the older labs cut some of their fees to hold on to their clients. Bill decided that he had to launch a new marketing campaign and advertise discounts that equaled his competitors'—but he never had the chance. A few weeks later, while on vacation in Wyoming with some old college friends, he was killed in a hunting accident.

Bill's son Eric, a 33-year-old advertising executive in Los Angeles, was named executor of the estate and left with the task of dealing with the lab's $250,000 debt. He also had to find a way to immediately meet the clinic's $75,000 of outstanding payments to doctors and suppliers. Eric's short-term aim was to keep the clinic in good standing since it was a consistent source of revenue. So his first major decision was to use the proceeds of an $80,000 insurance policy payable to the estate to retire the clinic's debt.

His next aim was to develop a long-term strategy to prevent the lab's debt from becoming unmanageable. He really only had two options: to sell everything or to sell the pharmacy and hold on to the lab and clinic. Clearly, the most practical option was to sell everything. Total liquidation would give his mother a half- million-dollar retirement fund that would pay her a handsome yearly income. The second option was very risky. Since no one else in the family had any business experience (Esthelle was a voice coach and Pamela and Vanya were nurses), Eric would have to quit his job and stay in Tucson for at least a year to manage the clinic and make the lab into a going concern. He would have to hope that he could get re-established in the advertising field at a later point. He would also have to hope that he could learn the medical business quickly enough to turn the lab around.

Eric was angry that his father had left the family in such a mess. Bill didn't have a comprehensive estate plan and didn't carry adequate insurance to cover debts; he hadn't planned for an untimely death. Eric was also angered that the family should find its business assets, which had always been rock solid, eroded by debt. To make up for the mistakes that led to this moment, Eric felt that he had to try to save the business.

Upon taking over the role of manager, Eric's first move was to sell the pharmacy. No one wanted to buy the business itself, given its declining revenue and the presence of the new chain. Nonetheless, he was able to sell the store property for close to its estimated value of $500,000. After deducting payables to creditors of his father's estate, including lawyers' and accountants' fees, funeral expenses and his executor fees, he recovered around $400,000. He used $250,000 of this amount to pay off the lab debt and the remaining $150,000 to pay out bequests of $50,000 to himself and each of his siblings, as specified in his father's will. The family now held its business assets debt-free and Eric was able to live off the income from the clinic ($30,000 per year). But his mother didn't have a secure source of income; she would have to eat into her retirement fund to survive. Their hope was that the lab would take off before the fund was exhausted.

Sadly, almost two years later, the picture had not substantially improved. Eric was able to get the lab to a yearly break-even point. However, the clinic faced competition from new clinics in the area and, consequently, revenue remained static. By this time, Esthelle had spent the last dollar of her retirement capital. To bail out his mother, Eric was forced to sell the clinic and the lab for $200,000, which he invested for his mother in bonds and mutual funds. Yet the income generated by this portfolio (around $20,000 a year) wouldn't be enough for his mother to live on comfortably. This meant Eric immediately had to find another high-paying job in advertising that would allow him to supplement his mother's income. Unfortunately, after being out of the industry for over two years in an unrelated field, Eric had a tough time getting reestablished. He eventually found a job with a small firm in Tucson but it was a big step down in pay and responsibility. He would be able to assist his mother but only by sacrificing his own financial dreams.

Eric fouled up his career and his family's inheritance because he couldn't stand the idea of presiding over a sinking ship. If his pride in his family's financial standing and his anger at his father's business and estate-planning errors hadn't been so intense, he would not have felt the need to take the risks entailed in trying to rescue the family business. Unfortunately, many inheritors who are left to pick up the pieces of an estate dashed by fate suffer the same lapse of practical judgment that Eric Taylor did.

## 5. The Honor-Thy-Father-and-Mother Syndrome

If you inherit a family business, especially one that spans more than one generation, you will certainly feel compelled to keep it in the family. That's fine, as long as you have the training, interest and inclination to run it. Obviously, if you don't have these qualities and you assume a managerial role, you may very well make bad decisions that sink the business. And, by the way, heirs of family businesses often find themselves in that situation. But why would anyone who doesn't know enough, or in some cases care enough, about the family business try to run it? One possible reason is guilt. You might say to yourself, "I couldn't live with myself if I sold Dad's company; it meant so much to him." Another reason is gratitude: "Mom was so generous in leaving me the business; I owe it to her to carry on with it." These motives can overwhelm practical judgment and lead an inheritor down the path to financial ruin. They can also lead to a career disaster if you leave a promising position for a family job that you don't really want.

I don't provide a case study for this syndrome because the previous case of Eric Taylor effectively illustrates the problem. Just imagine that Eric had decided to run the clinic and lab from a feeling of guilt or gratitude rather than anger and you get the same result. A young man loses the family business because he didn't understand it and at the same time loses tremendous opportunities in the field he abandoned.

# 6. The Home-Alone Syndrome

It's an unfortunate fact that friends and acquaintances are often critical, unsupportive or distant because they resent your inheritance. In particular, some may try to make you feel guilty about receiving unearned wealth. As a result, you might find yourself at home, alone, watching television because you don't have anyone with whom you can discuss the demands and problems posed by your situation. If the criticism has been extreme, breaking out of this isolation can be difficult. It might so diminish your sense of self-worth that you lack the confidence to go out and meet new people, believing that they too are likely to judge you harshly.

The battle against isolation can become even more difficult if you inherit a substantial estate that makes you financially self-sufficient. You might decide to give up your accustomed way of life, including your job, and seek out alternatives. Paradoxically, you might find loneliness and longing rather than a way of life that has spiritual satisfaction. When you are in the unique position of calling your own shots, in a world where almost no one has the same privilege, you'll have trouble finding new friends and colleagues, as well as holding on to the old ones.

Some of these problems are reflected in our next case study, which explains how Martha, a single 48-year-old librarian from a small city in Maine, found herself alone at home after receiving a substantial bequest.

Martha and her father, the retired owner of a GM dealership, lived on the same block in a small residential area in the middle of their little community, which had a population of around 30,000. Since Martha's brother was based in Europe with the armed forces and her younger sister was married and living in Texas, she was responsible for taking care of her father, who had been in poor health for a number of years. She visited him at home every day, often made his dinner and arranged for outside help for him on a regular basis. Out of gratitude, he amended his will shortly before his death and made her his principal beneficiary, leaving her a half-million dollars in stock.

Having had no previous financial experience, other than socking her savings away in a retirement plan, she wasn't quite sure what to do with her bequest. And she experienced serious difficulty in finding someone to advise her. She couldn't talk to her friends at the public library, none of whom had ever had access to that kind of money. They also did a good job of alienating her when they took to calling her Princess Martha after hearing the local gossip that her father had left her a considerable sum. She couldn't rely on her two or three close friends outside of work for advice because they had no experience in the world of business. The estate's executor, a local lawyer, tried to help by referring Martha to a couple of brokers in town. However, Martha wasn't inclined to trust local advisors since she knew that she couldn't expect confidentiality in a city where gossip was a way of life. She had also already received the hard sell from some local businesspeople who were looking for capital, and she had hated it. She wanted to avoid further hassles at all cost.

Isolated from everyone around her, Martha decided to just leave the stocks alone for the time being, carry on with her job at the library and collect her dividends. That was fine for a couple of years until the market got a little rocky and she lost $150,000 over the course of about three months. That loss goaded her to action. She took a two-week vacation and went to Bangor, where she interviewed financial planners and consultants. Eventually she found a woman she felt she could trust. Winona Winter, who specialized in retirement planning, was a former banker with a conservative outlook. Winona recommended diversification and introduced Martha to an affiliated broker who was willing to play it safe. He invested her portfolio, which had been heavily oriented toward large manufacturing concerns in the auto industry, in a stable mix of bonds (30 percent), mortgages (30 percent) and mutual funds (40 percent).

In the end, Martha's mutual funds did quite well and in a few years she had recouped some of her losses. Martha had broken out of her isolation and sought the right kind of professional assistance before she suffered unrecoverable losses. If you find yourself in her situation, follow suit.

# 7. The Oedipus Syndrome

A person with an Oedipus complex is someone who is attracted to his mother to the point that he becomes jealous of his father and has thoughts of supplanting him. (The ancient Greek myth of Oedipus tells the story of a young man who marries his mother and kills his father.) I use the term "Oedipus Syndrome" to refer to the way in which intergenerational jealousy can cause someone to mismanage a parent's estate. If you lived in the shadow of an overachieving parent whose life you envied in some way, you might use your family inheritance to try to exceed your parent's accomplishments. When the primary aim is to be richer or a more formidable businessperson than your parent, you might make dangerous high-risk investments or indulge in reckless quixotism. Consider how the billionaire Hunt brothers lost everything when they tried to corner the silver market. Jaclyn Fierman of *Fortune* magazine reports:

> *Anxious to outdo their daddy, a wheeler-dealer in the oil patch, Nelson Bunker and William Herbert Hunt of Dallas began hoarding silver in the early 70s. When the market collapsed in 1980, they borrowed $1.1 billion to meet margin calls, borrowings they secured with oil assets. Mistake No. 2. Oil prices plunged, and their company filed for Chapter 11.*[3]

In our next case study, I introduce you to the Cafritz family of Washington, D.C., a wealthy clan whose actions were so astonishing that they reached the front page of the *Washington Post* in the late 1980s.

Morris Cafritz, who had been D.C.'s most successful developer and one of its wealthiest citizens, died in 1964. He willed one-half of his estate to a trust he and his wife had established in 1948, the Morris and Gwendolyn Cafritz Foundation, which supported a wide range of charitable and artistic endeavors. One-quarter went to his wife in a marital trust, and the remaining quarter went to his three sons, Conrad, Carter and Calvin.[4] This arrangement was later altered when the sons had a dispute with their mother about the disposal of another trust that had been set up by their father during his lifetime. A settlement was reached that stipulated the sons would get one-quarter of the marital trust upon their mother's death in return for which they would forfeit some of the monies in the disputed trust. This agreement was still in force when Gwendolyn Cafritz died in November of 1988, leaving an estate valued at around $140 million with over half that amount, about $84 million, sitting in the marital trust. Each son was to receive $7 million from the trust tax-free since all estate taxes had already been paid by their father's estate. The rest of the trust, some $60 million, and the other assets, worth about $56 million, were left to the foundation.[5]

In spite of the fact that each son had already become a multimillionaire by following Cafritz Sr. into the world of real estate,[6] and each was taking another $7 million tax-free to boot, the two younger sons, Conrad (age 50) and Carter (age 52), decided to contest their mother's will. They pleaded that the estate's executors, former Secretary of State William Rogers, who had been Gwendolyn's lawyer and a director of the board of the foundation for decades, and Martin Atlas, a long-time business adviser to the family and also a director of the board, had persuaded Mrs. Cafritz, while in an enfeebled state of mind, to leave most of her estate to the foundation. The brothers asserted that their mother lacked the capacity to execute her new will and that she had signed it under pressure from Rogers and Atlas, who had exercised "undue influence." For these reasons, they asked to have the will set aside.[7]

Marjorie Williams, who covered this story for the *Washington Post Magazine*, asked the question that had to be on the minds of many Washingtonians:

> What do Conrad and Carter Cafritz hope to gain from an arduous legal proceeding that already involves at least 12 law firms and threatens to stretch on for years? None of the Cafritz can be said to need the money that is at stake. All are multimillionaires, and Conrad Cafritz, by most accounts the prime instigator of the lawsuit, has spun his inheritance from his father into a vast personal fortune of at minimum $100 million.[8]

Williams speculates on the possible motives. Since Mrs. Cafritz was a minority owner of some of her late husband's real estate holdings, the balance being held by the foundation, the sons might have wanted her share in order to become players in the management of their father's empire. (The foundation held over $220 million in assets.) On the other hand, they might have wanted to control the foundation. Since Conrad and Carter had never been appointed to the board, they might have been using the suit to bargain for the right to serve as directors or control the nomination of the board's president. In this case, their aims would be to use the foundation to exploit business opportunities and to support causes that reflected their own visions of social change. Either motive would be consistent with the syndrome of intergenerational jealousy.

If they could add their mother's assets to their own considerable wealth, and at the same time control their father's assets by controlling the foundation, they would have enough power to outdo their father in the financial world and outdo their mother in the social world, where her control of the foundation, as well as her own ambitions, had made her the maven of Washington high society. (The social power may have been particularly attractive to Conrad, who was a well-known supporter of liberal causes.) This conclusion is supported by Williams' suggestion that the sons contested the will because they didn't want their mother to have the "last word." This, of course, implies that they also didn't want their father to have the last word, since controlling their mother's legacy was the key to controlling his.

In the end, of course, we can't say with certitude what really motivated Conrad and Carter Cafritz. They might have really believed that Rogers and Atlas wanted to control the foundation and had manipulated their mother to that end. The *Post* account also invites us to consider that their behavior might have been a response to their stormy relationship with their mother, which was in evidence as early as 1964 when they challenged her control of one of the trusts. It was rumored that her drinking habits had played a major role in causing the disaffection of her sons. When they inherited less than they anticipated, they may have felt that their mother had tried to settle the score by, in effect, disinheriting them. (Remember that their share of the marital trust was the product of the 1964 trust settlement, not Mrs. Cafritz's will.) In this case, their contestation of the will might have been a destructive example of what I referred to previously as the I'm-Too-Worthy Syndrome. Feeling they deserved more than they received, Conrad and Carter embarked on a costly attempt to settle the score by pleading for the courts to give them more.

Assuming for our purposes that the Cafritz boys were suffering from the Oedipus Syndrome, their example is worth keeping in mind. It illustrates in caricatured form how wealth can inspire harmful ambitions instead of providing a peaceful reprieve from the competition for power after power, as the television lottery ads would have us believe.

# 8. The Great-Expectations Syndrome

If you've grown up in a family that has a long tradition of achievement, financial or otherwise, you may feel that you have to do great things to justify ownership of the family name. In fact, you may have been told by family members that you are expected to do great things. Rather than inspiring envy of successful family members, which is what creates the desire to exceed their works (the Oedipus Syndrome), an impressive family tradition can inspire a fear that, unless you equal your family's achievements, you will be deemed a failure. This can drive someone to risk an inheritance on a momentous enterprise that isn't commercially viable. Keeping up with the Joneses can be risky and burdensome, especially, as our next case study demonstrates, when you're one of them.

Oscar Jones came from a long line of athletes and businesspeople on his father's side of the family and a long line of professionals on his mother's side, all of whom came from Illinois. His great-grandfather on his father's side had founded at the beginning of the century a small auto company, which his grandfather had later transformed into an auto parts plant that produced interior accessories for Ford. His father, Virgil, who had been a football standout at Michigan, decided to make his name in the insurance business and had used revenue from the plant to establish a regional network of home and auto insurance offices. To keep the plant running smoothly while he pursued his own dreams, Virgil had wisely chosen a trusted senior employee, Rico, to manage the plant. With the assistance of the family's accountant, who was also an experienced entrepreneur, Rico kept the plant operating at full capacity most of the time.

Oscar's maternal relatives had also distinguished themselves in the business world. His grandfather had been involved in the export of agricultural products and was one of the founding members of the Chicago Board of Trade. His mother had used the family's money to become a driving force behind a number of local charities and was well-known in Chicago for her work in supporting the arts. Her most recent project was the formation of a new organization devoted to preserving historic buildings in North Chicago.

The Joneses employed a double standard in raising Oscar and his two older sisters. His sisters weren't expected to go into business or take up a profession. One studied fine art at the University of Chicago and became an assistant curator at a museum in San Francisco; the other studied English at Chicago Loyola, married shortly after graduation and moved to Ohio; where she was raising a family. On the other hand, from an early age, Oscar had been raised to succeed in business. He was expected to take over the parts plant and take the helm of his father's little insurance empire. After graduating from Cornell with a degree in business, Oscar returned to Chicago and at the tender age of 23 took on managerial responsibilities at the plant.

One of the major factors in the plant's continued success had been the efficiency of the managerial team. By elevating Rico, who had worked on the line for close to 25 years, to the position of manager, Virgil had ensured that the management team would remain small. The employees trusted Rico, who walked the tightrope of representing management while acting as an effective advocate of employee concerns. In effect, he had become both manager and union leader of the unorganized workplace. This meant there was no need for a proliferation of executive positions. The management team consisted of Virgil, who performed an oversight function; the family's accountant, who handled all financial matters; and the plant's three engineers, one of whom was responsible for keeping the lines of communication open with Ford. Virgil had been practicing lean management before the term was ever invented.

Over the next four years, Virgil, now in his mid-50s, reduced his involvement in his companies and spent much of his time yachting on the Great Lakes during the summer and in the Caribbean during the winter. (He eventually sold the insurance business to one of his partners.) At the same time, he allowed Oscar to gradually take over the top managerial spot at the plant and ease Rico into retirement. When Oscar acceded to the post of president and general manager, the plant employed close to 150 employees. Though his son was only 27 years old, Virgil was confident that he would succeed stupendously; after all, he had been born to rule.

Oscar's mettle was soon tested by the competitive pressures placed on the auto industry by the Japanese automakers who were gaining a serious foothold in North America. As Detroit looked desperately for ways to improve quality control, Ford was the first automaker to follow the Japanese example and place stringent control requirements on key suppliers. This included the Jones plant. Ford gave Oscar a 12-month deadline to substantially improve his products or it would find another supplier at the end of the current two-year contract. Oscar was panic-stricken by the thought that he might lose the Ford account, which had been the lifeblood of the business since his grandfather's days. His first knee-jerk reaction was to deal with the crisis on his own. Admitting that he needed his father, Rico or the family accountant, whose cost-control function Oscar had assigned to a computer program, would be to admit that he wasn't the crack businessman his family expected him to be. His second knee-jerk reaction was to deal with the problem bureaucratically, as any good manager would. He hired three new managers, all with MBAs, who would be responsible for reorganizing the manufacturing process, instilling a new set of values in the employees and instituting strict measures of product improvement.

Ten months later, his team wasn't doing too well. Managerial overhead had quadrupled and was cutting into the revenue needed to finance the retooling of the plant. The team scrapped Rico's egalitarian leadership with a top-down management style that alienated employees and made them unreceptive to the company's new techniques and ideals. The team itself was young and inexperienced, which led to many false starts and delays in implementing new production methods. (Fearing that older managers would usurp his role, Oscar had hired recent graduates of MBA programs, believing they would be more receptive to his leadership.) All these problems led to a failure to meet basic Ford benchmarks in the twelfth month. Ford gave notice that it would not renew its contract at the end of the following year.

Oscar's crack management team scrambled. They convinced Oscar to draw down on cash reserves to make additional improvements with the aim of achieving tolerances that would allow them to compete for contracts with Japanese automakers. And they turned out to be right. The new changes did produce impressive results, which led to promises of long-term contracts from Toyota. But there was one catch: The contracts were so large that Oscar would have to build a second plant to meet increasing production targets.

With the conditional contracts in hand, Oscar approached his banker, who floated loans to cover the construction of the new plant, which would be up and running before the Ford contract expired. With financing in place, Oscar won the Toyota contracts. He was ecstatic at the prospect of simultaneously rescuing and expanding the business. He was about to exceed his family's great expectations for his career.

Then an unforeseen event changed everything. After a year and a half of struggling against the new management style, the employees were so disaffected that they allowed the Teamsters to unionize the plant. That brought a demand for increased salaries and, eventually, a strike. The Teamster representatives advised the employees to strike before the new plant was finished so they would be assured of sharing in the company's future prosperity. Unfortunately, the month-long strike and the final wage settlement had such a drastic impact on company revenue that the bank was forced to call its loan. By the time Oscar and his team found alternative financing, they were so far behind in building the new plant that they missed their production deadline and lost the Toyota contract. Jones Manufacturing was forced to declare bankruptcy.

The way in which Oscar Jones' family prepared him to accept the responsibility of managing his grandfather's business guaranteed that he would fail in the process. By being burdened with too much wealth and responsibility at a young age and expectations to live up to the punishing standard set by his forebears, as well as by his father, Oscar was destined to fail. He reacted to the pressure of great expectations by trying to do it all on his own, and that in turn led to errors of judgment that defeated those expectations. If he had consulted with Rico and the family accountant, he would have learned that a low-key management style had always been the secret to the success of the plant. Armed with that insight, he might very well have avoided the union drive that finally defeated him.

## 9. The Family-Secrets Syndrome

An inheritance sometimes reveals secrets that can forever change your view of your parent, grandparent or relative. From the estate accounts you might learn that a deceased parent had much less money than he claimed, or much more. Business records might disclose an unsavory deal or a venture, otherwise portrayed as successful, on the verge of bankruptcy. A will might name a mysterious beneficiary who turns out to be a lover on the side or an out-of-wedlock child. A grandparent's bias in favor of or against a grandchild might be revealed by a will that distributes assets unequally. Hurtful revelations like these force you to reconsider whether your benefactor really deserved your love and respect. Unquestioning affection can give way to feelings of ambivalence and anger. When that happens, you might be tempted to punish your benefactor for his or her offense by wasting the assets. So it was with Judy Blumstock.

Judy's father, Monty, had been one of Montreal's most well-known lawyers, building a successful solo practice from scratch over a period of 30 years. Judy and her brother, Mark, had been raised in affluence but their father had scrupulously avoided discussing his business affairs in their presence. Monty had placed great importance on the sanctity of family life and refused to allow his professional activities to usurp his private life. So, when he died at the age of 66, his family was surprised, in spite of his long career in practice, to find that he had accumulated investments and property valued at more than $1.7 million. He left $500,000 in bonds and T-bills to be split equally between Judy, who had just turned 33 and had recently been elevated to an executive position in a telecommunications company based in the city, and Mark, a local commercial Realtor. The rest of his estate was bequeathed to his wife, Marci.

About six weeks after Monty's death, while preparations were being made for probate, Mark unexpectedly paid Judy a visit at her apartment one evening and dropped a bombshell. That afternoon he had spoken to the family's lawyer, who had informed him that the estate was being investigated by federal tax authorities (Revenue Canada). The investigation, which had begun prior to their father's death, had focused on corporate transactions with a known underworld figure who had been one of Monty's clients. Revenue Canada suspected that Monty had not declared some of the fees for these transactions and had placed them, or the client had placed them, in a foreign tax haven. Mark had been advised that members of the family should refer any questions posed directly by federal officials to their lawyer.

After a year-long inquiry into Monty's affairs, Revenue Canada ruled that some of the income diverted to the tax haven should have been declared in Canada. The estate was forced to pay $400,000 in back taxes and penalties; $100,000 was paid from the children's shares (thus reducing each bequest to $200,000) and the rest came from Marci's share.

Obviously, the Blumstocks were still very well-off in spite of the ruling. After paying off the fine and using the funds in the foreign account to pay the estate taxes, Monty's estate was still worth $1.4 million. Emotionally, though, the family was hurting. They all felt betrayed by Monty. His honesty and integrity, which had been hallmarks in his professional and private lives, were now in doubt. If he had conspired with a criminal to defraud the government, what other frauds might he have perpetrated on clients, friends or family?

In Judy's case, these ambivalent feelings played themselves out in the management of her inheritance. Thinking that her share might also represent ill-gotten gain, she decided to give it away to conservative causes that her liberal father would never have supported. This allowed her to absolve herself of guilt about receiving tainted money and to punish her father posthumously for his wrongdoing.

However, a year later, when she needed extra cash to make a down payment on her first home, Judy started to regret her decision to give away her inheritance. After all, she couldn't say for sure that her share had been tainted; maybe the fine paid to Revenue Canada had fully rectified every impropriety. In the end, she felt that she had actually punished herself. That's when she sought out a therapist who would help her learn to forgive her father for his failings and forgive herself for giving away his money.

\* \* \*

In the last two chapters, the subjects of our case studies suffered a loss of self-esteem, a loss that, for some, proved to be more vexing than their monetary losses. They punished themselves by attributing their mistakes to moral or intellectual weakness; they were also punished by family, friends and casual observers who offered the same criticism. And that is unfortunate, because, as we've seen, that criticism often doesn't get to the truth about a loss. We often have trouble recognizing that poor judgment in dealing with an inheritance can be the result of a symptom of grief or a symptom of affluence. Once we realize this, we can begin to restore ourselves financially and psychologically. We can avoid further losses by waiting for our symptoms to resolve themselves or adopting a strategy, perhaps in consultation with a therapist, for resolving them. At the same time, we can renew self-confidence because we understand that a mistake resulted from transient symptoms rather than a defect of character.

# How to Give and Take Bad Advice

Grief always takes you by surprise. You can't imagine (because you don't want to imagine) how you'll feel after losing a parent, sibling, relative or friend. Even when you know the end is near and think you're prepared, the moment of loss can hit you like a sucker-punch. You may be comforted in the difficult days that follow by the knowledge that your friend or family member has moved from one world to the next. However, that comfort will be short-lived unless you understand how your life has been drastically changed by your loss. The world of the survivor is, in some sense, also a new world. You have just lost someone who played a key role in providing advice and determining your judgments. You may also lose supporters among friends, family members and professionals as a result of your bereavement. In this chapter, I want to show you that you must find new friends and experts if you hope to manage an inheritance effectively.

As we've seen, this new world of bereavement is populated with a host of foreign emotions that can lead anyone to mismanage an inheritance. This world also contains other problems that can interfere with the effective management of an estate: isolation, changes among supporters and poor estate planning.

Losing a family member or close friend will deprive you of the advice and support you so badly need to manage the inheritance that he or she has left you. Suddenly, Dad is no longer there to give advice about purchasing a home or evaluating a new job opportunity; you can't turn to Mom for the encouragement and moral support that got you through so many tough times; your creative off-the-wall business ideas are no longer tempered by the flinty criticisms of your best friend and business partner; your sister isn't around to keep you focused on your most important needs and goals.

Unfortunately, you may regard the loss of a family member, particularly a parent, as a rite of passage that entitles you to make key decisions independently. This may prevent you from realizing that you must go through a long period of adjustment to learn how to make important financial decisions on your own, and that, in the short term, your loss will rob you of sound practical judgment.

Changes among key supporters can also have a profound impact on your judgment. The crisis of personal loss often changes the circle of family and friends on whom you rely for comfort and sound advice. Obviously, any personal crisis, especially one caused by bereavement, gives you an opportunity to find out who your real friends are. Some of your lukewarm friends will turn out to be your strongest supporters, and some of your closest friends will turn out to be lukewarm supporters.

Unfortunately, a bereavement can bring out the worst in some people. Many of my clients have been surprised to see how many friends backed off and watched them sink under the weight of personal loss and estate problems. This can happen for any number of reasons. Some friends may feel so threatened by your hardship that they can cope only by ignoring it; they don't want to be reminded that your misery could easily be theirs some day.[1] Others may not know how to extend help to a grieving person. To avoid saying or doing the wrong thing, they withdraw. Friends of the deceased may themselves be so traumatized by the loss that they can't reach out to help you. Those who do help may give up in frustration when their efforts do not alleviate your distress and depression.[2]

As we saw in Chapter 4 under the Home-Alone Syndrome, others may simply be envious that you have inherited something and take the attitude that you don't need help because you've got money. Finally, those who offer inappropriate support may seem to have abandoned you even as they try to help. Supposedly comforting words, such as "I know how you feel," "Don't worry, you have a lot to look forward to," "It's natural to be upset at a time like this," can be worse than no help at all. These comments can trivialize your plight by making you feel that your problems are somehow normal and not deserving of special respect.[3] Also, within the family, particularly when a parent is lost, relationships may shift dramatically. An older sibling who isn't equipped to lead may assume a leadership role; siblings may feud over the division of inherited possessions; a widowed parent may soon remarry and bring a "stranger" into the family.

As you lose important supporters and gain new ones, you may be lost in confusion as you try to sort out new opinions and perspectives when making decisions about the management of your inheritance. You will need time to learn who you can rely on for sound financial and personal advice.

The other problem that most inheritors face is poor estate planning. It results from the fact that most benefactors cannot foresee the world that their beneficiaries will face without them. Some benefactors try to provide for their family and friends by means of estate planning and a carefully drafted will. Nonetheless, even the most far-sighted person will have trouble foreseeing all the potential problems that can arise when he or she is no longer there to affect the outcome. The reason is simple: A will and an estate plan are based on a forecast, aspects of which will inevitably be wrong. How was your father, who died in 1988 at the peak of the real estate boom, to foresee that the commercial property he left you would devalue so quickly in 1990 that you would have to sell it? How could your mother, who left her interest-bearing assets to your brother, the underpaid teacher, foresee that you would lose your lucrative job in the world of finance when downsizing eliminated your department? How could your grandfather, who left you funds that could be used only for a college education, foresee that his only granddaughter would forgo college to raise a family?

A prescient person might provide in his will that his beneficiary or beneficiaries rely on certain trusted friends and advisers for assistance on important financial and estate matters. That may alleviate some of the problems ensuing from the isolation and shifting relationships that can skew an inheritor's judgments. However, most wills won't recognize these problems because most benefactors can't really imagine the world *ex post facto*.

We can now see what a devastating effect the loss of one person can have on an inheritor's ability to manage a bequest. Not only must an inheritor suffer from poor judgment stemming from the symptoms of grief, but he may also find that his judgment is further clouded by the consequences of personal loss—isolation, changes among supporters, and estate planning that almost always turns out to be deficient. The stress of these combined problems can drive any inheritor to the brink of losing all powers of sound practical judgment and thereby undermine his ability to effectively manage his or her inheritance.

Sadly, grief and the other consequences of personal loss often prevent an inheritor from seeking out the right friends and advisers until disaster strikes. Sometimes we can learn to manage an inheritance only after mismanaging it to the point of almost losing it. It's not a very comforting thought. Every inheritor needs friends and advisers to help him or her see the things that must be done to preserve and enhance the bequest. However, grief and all the problems that follow it will also rob an inheritor of the sound judgment that's needed to find people who can be trusted. Bereavement places an inheritor in a Chinese box in which every path leads to a dead end.

In pointing out this dilemma, my intention is not to discourage you from trying to deal effectively with your inheritance. Rather, I want to make you aware of this dilemma to give you an opportunity to think your way out of it.

How can you find the right friends and advisers to assist you in managing an inheritance when everything often seems stacked against your finding them? The first step is to distinguish between friends and experts; that is, between those who can provide personal advice and those who can provide professional advice. Some simple definitions will help us here. An expert is someone who knows something you don't and can charge you a lot of money to tell you what it is. The job of the expert, whether a lawyer, an accountant or a banker, is to provide detached, carefully reasoned advice that will solve your estate problems. The expert's role is to ensure that the management of your inheritance is governed by objective considerations. Have you complied with the terms of your benefactor's will? Have you complied with the relevant legislation governing wills and trusts? Have you calculated your tax liabilities properly? Have you considered converting some securities to avoid losing money in volatile markets?

A friend, on the other hand, is someone who knows something that can help you and shares it with you freely. A friend's job is to provide advice that speaks to your private needs and beliefs. His or her role is to ensure that personal considerations also govern the management of your inheritance.

From my own experiences and those of my clients, I have found that the helplessness and confusion that follow a bereavement are often expressed by looking for advice in the wrong places. You may try to get expert advice from a friend or personal advice from an expert. In either case, you're heading for trouble.

When you trust a friend to advise on tough personal questions, you may also be tempted to look to that person for advice that only a professional can provide. Some friends may be all too willing, with good intentions, to give you the benefit of their insights into real estate, stocks, auctions and other financial matters. Just as bereavement can bring out the worst in some of your friends, it can also bring out the "best." Their helpful advice may turn out to be harmful.

Consider the case of a young woman, Charlotte, who inherited a $300,000 stock portfolio from her father, a highly successful farm equipment salesman, who suffered a fatal heart attack in 1987. Although she was originally from a small town in Alberta, for the past three years she had been living in Toronto, where she was doing an apprenticeship with a hair stylist in the hope of opening her own salon one day. When several of her closest friends learned of her windfall, they advised her to cash in the stocks and buy a small home in the downtown area. Her older friends, who had seen their home values skyrocket during the 1980s, believed that home ownership would be the best investment Charlotte could ever make. Her younger friends, who didn't own homes, saw an opportunity for Charlotte to get into a market they couldn't afford to enter. They were all sure that she couldn't lose with real estate in the middle of a growing metropolis while the stock market, they warned, was unpredictable, an opinion confirmed by the losses she took on Black Monday.

Trusting her friends, Charlotte hastily invested in a $250,000 unrenovated duplex in a fashionable district. She was able to make a $200,000 cash payment by selling most of her blue-chip stocks and mutual funds and took a small mortgage of $50,000 to cover the balance of the purchase price. She planned to use the interest income from the remaining $100,000 in her portfolio and her salary as a stylist to pay down the mortgage over a five-year term. Then the recession hit. The real estate market plummeted, causing the value of her home to drop by 25 percent, she lost her job as a hair stylist when her boss went bankrupt, and her remaining stocks dropped in value by $40,000. She had trouble finding work and, in the meantime, had to encroach on her dwindling portfolio to meet her mortgage payments and living expenses. Within a year her portfolio had been reduced to $30,000, a sum that generated a mere $2,800 in income on a yearly basis; as a result, she was forced to sell her new home at the bottom of the market. She received $180,000 for a home that she had purchased a year before for a quarter of a million dollars. After the real estate commission and the bank's mortgage were paid out, she was left with approximately $130,000. Adding this sum to Charlotte's $30,000 in stocks left her with a net worth of $160,000. In less than a year, good friends had helped Charlotte squander almost half of her inheritance.

Charlotte should have been advised to avoid investing in real estate in an inflated market (a better bet, of course, is to buy at the bottom, not the top) and to get some solid advice from a stockbroker and an accountant on how to preserve and enhance her stock portfolio. Since she was just embarking on a new career and had no assurances of continuing employment and no personal savings, she needed her investment income to keep her afloat until she was established in her field. By taking the advice of friends and buying a home that she really didn't need (she wasn't married and wasn't planning on having children in the near future), she compromised the financial security that her father had hoped his portfolio would provide, at a time when she sorely needed it.

As this example illustrates, people tend to give advice that simply reflects their own needs and beliefs. Giving advice is an art. It requires the adviser to see things from your perspective, not his or hers. Psychiatrists and psychologists spend a lifetime learning to dispense advice that speaks to someone's true interests. However, even they fail to understand and help some people, and among themselves continue to differ on methods and interpretations of behavior. You'll be lucky if you can find that rare friend who can see what's really best *for you*.

Another problem with helpful friends is that they can be much more influential than they ever wanted to be, if you let them. You may make the mistake of treating personal advice as professional advice and place undue weight on their opinions. When you are grieving, you may find temporary security or solace in a piece of friendly advice that was offered casually and isn't really that helpful. Beware of that fellow who takes you aside and says, "Just remember one word: plastics."

Let me illustrate this point with another case study. One of my clients, Richard, a construction foreman in his late 30s, had inherited a number of possessions from his mother's estate, including a crystal collection. Richard had always admired the collection, which his mother had proudly displayed in the living room of their family home, but he had never considered whether he would enjoy having it or whether it had monetary value. So he was a bit surprised when he received it. When he told a couple of close friends about the pieces, they casually suggested that he sell them. After all, Richard was a rough-and-tumble kind of guy who enjoyed hockey, football and muscle cars. He really wouldn't enjoy showing off his crystal vases to his beer-drinking buddies. He'd be better off selling and putting the proceeds toward an overhaul of the high-powered engine in his Dodge Charger. Leading such an active life, Richard didn't have much time to consider what to do with the crystal collection. And since other family members lived on the West Coast, he didn't bother to seek out their advice. So, one day, with his friends still exerting influence by default, he sent the collection to a local auction house and sold it for $2,000. That tidy sum allowed him to pay for the overhaul. He was ecstatic...for a while.

When his sister Marge flew in from San Diego for a weekend visit two weeks later and learned that he had sold the collection, she was appalled. She told him that their mother had held on to the collection as an investment. Apparently, it included several pieces by the famed French artist, René Lalique. Marge said that Mom had never had the collection evaluated but had assumed that it was worth at least $20,000. When the will had been read, Marge had avoided talking to her brother about the collection because she felt it would have been in bad taste to discuss the value of possessions so soon after the funeral. She also assumed that Richard would hold on to the collection for sentimental reasons.

Before acting on the advice of his friends, Richard should have consulted at least two, and preferably three, auction or antique dealers who were experienced with French crystal. With correct evaluations, he would have learned that he owned expensive objects that would only increase in value, and perhaps he would have held on to them. Even if he had decided to sell, at least he would have received enough money to make a secure long-term investment, a result that would have been consistent with his mother's original intention in collecting French crystal.

Even when friends don't offer "expert" advice, they can create problems by leading you to place too much emphasis on personal considerations when you're trying to make tough decisions about the management of an inheritance.

This point brings to mind the case of the misguided widow. Betty Farnsworth was in her 50s when her husband, a prominent architect in Philadelphia, passed away. After spending 30 years organizing her life around her husband's professional and social activities, and with her two children living in Houston, she found herself in a vacuum. Friends started to worry when Betty was still sequestered in the family home months after the funeral. Several friends urged Betty to sell her home as the first step in starting a new life. Apparently, they felt the home was so associated with her past life that it prevented her from thinking about the future.

Betty took the advice to heart and sold the home, but without having any clear idea of what she wanted to do with the rest of her life. Eventually, she joined her sister in Brussels, where she had spent her teens and early 20s, in the hope of finding some concrete direction. After spending almost a year cloistered in her sister's home, Betty returned to Philadelphia, only to find that she could no longer afford to buy a home in her old neighborhood. Prices were skyrocketing, and on the advice of an incompetent stockbroker, who also happened to be her nephew, she had recently lost a great deal of money on the market. Betty spent the rest of her life regretting the decision to sell her precious family home, which her husband had taken so much pride in designing.

If Betty had taken professional advice before she embarked on her European adventure, she would have fared much better. A competent real estate appraiser would have advised her to hold on to her home while prices continued to rise. She could have leased the home to finance her move to Belgium and sold later only if she was sure that she didn't want to return. Obviously, she also needed a better stockbroker who would have advised her to invest in a safer mix of securities so she wouldn't have to worry about the ups and downs of the market while dealing with her personal problems.

In the end, all these examples show us that when a friend offers financial advice, you should take it with a grain of salt. Then seek independent advice from a qualified expert.

Now let's turn to the problems with experts. Unless an expert is a long-time family friend or a therapist, generally he or she isn't equipped to give personal advice. The expert operates in the realm of rules, figures and market forces. He or she isn't concerned about your personal situation and isn't trained to evaluate it. An expert who tries to give personal advice usually gives bad advice. Your lawyer or your accountant can't tell you whether you'll sleep well if you sell the family home, fight with your siblings over family possessions or collapse a retirement fund to buy a new car. Only a friend who understands your needs, aspirations and family history can address issues like these.

Unfortunately, the education of the modern expert has made it more likely that he or she is only qualified to give you purely technical advice, but also more likely that he or she will mistakenly give you personal advice. Let me explain: In the past, anyone who aspired to a learned profession would normally earn a bachelor's degree, often in the humanities, before going on to earn a technical degree at the graduate level. This ensured that every graduating professional had a solid general education in human affairs that would provide a certain wisdom about the role and limits of his or her specialized field. This kind of person was often referred to as the gentleman doctor, lawyer, etc. This expert was someone who could reflect on the political, social and moral ramifications of advice. With a bachelor's education, the expert at least had some training to think through the broader or deeper significance of the advice. If the gentleman lawyer mixed professional and personal advice, the client at least had some chance of receiving a thoughtful response on the personal side.

Today, however, even liberal education has become technical and specialized—specialized because arts faculties have mimicked the professions and require undergraduate students to master a narrow field so they can demonstrate expertise and relevance to potential employers, and technical because the arts curriculum is now dominated by courses that stress fact-gathering rather than the examination of beliefs and principles. The result is that those who go on to become professionals have received, from start to finish, a technical education that leads away from reflecting on the political, social or moral context in which they deliver advice to their clients. Paradoxically, though, these experts have overwhelming confidence in their expertise because it is so specialized and esoteric, and this often leads them to give personal advice that they aren't equipped to give. As John Ralston Saul has argued so persuasively in his recent work, *Voltaire's Bastards*, the experts' highly specialized knowledge has made them contemptuous of the very people they serve and all too ready to advise well beyond the scope of their training and understanding.

So, when dealing with experts, an inheritor is in a double bind. He must seek assistance from those whose knowledge is so specialized and complex that he cannot fully understand their advice. This forces him to place undue trust in the expert's ability to defend his interests. At the same time, this trust and the expert's tendency to advise on personal matters make the client vulnerable to receiving inappropriate and misguided advice.

Two other problems are worthy of note here. The first is that the demise of the gentleman expert has also been hastened by the development of large firms in burgeoning urban areas. Not long ago, when cities were smaller and cultural communities were more homogeneous, experts who grew up or lived in these communities would serve their members faithfully. They knew their clients personally and served them with an intimate knowledge of their tastes, beliefs and traditions. This arrangement ensured that professional advice was offered by someone who could be sensitive to the overall needs of his clients. Even if the community lawyer hadn't received a liberal education, he could still approximate the wisdom of the gentleman lawyer because he was so close to the people he served.[4]

Today, the community expert still exists in small towns; however, in larger centers, he's hard to find because cultural communities are less cohesive[5] and experts have organized themselves in large firms to attract regional, national and, in some cases, international business. The modern urban expert rarely bases his practice on an attachment to a community and its way of life. In this sense, he has become the perfect expert—he's totally independent and available to give unbiased advice to anyone. However, the perfect expert becomes imperfect for the same reason. He often doesn't understand his own clients, which is a real problem when he's dispensing advice that may radically alter their lives, for better or worse.

Needless to say, the personal biases of experts can also prevent them from giving good advice. Consider a client of mine whose life was thrown into confusion when he inherited a successful family business that went bankrupt under his management during the recent recession. I advised him to seek some professional counseling to deal with his personal and financial losses. He was referred by his doctor to a reputable psychiatrist. However, after a few weeks, the client was back in my office complaining about the therapist. The good doctor was at first quite helpful about the personal loss, but in later sessions was not at all sympathetic about the financial losses. My client found this very troubling. It had the effect of trivializing the terrible anguish he felt about his failure to save the family business. From comments the psychiatrist made at the last session about his own financial losses resulting from his recent divorce, my client realized that discussing his financial losses just hit too close to home for Doctor X. The doctor was having so much trouble facing his own losses that he couldn't face my client's. Experts are people, too, and you have to realize when their own problems prevent them from dealing properly with yours.

The true bottom line for any inheritor is to find a balance between professional and personal advice when deciding how to manage an inheritance. Acting on a professional recommendation (one that isn't simply dictated by law) that conflicts with personal advice that speaks to your most important needs or beliefs is one way to mismanage an inheritance; acting on a personal recommendation that conflicts with competent professional advice is another. So how do you know when you've reached the balance of views that defines good management of an estate? Finding the right answers to your estate problems requires a lengthy process of deliberation; there is no quick fix. Remember that the worst thing you can do is make an important decision concerning the management of your inheritance when you're still suffering from the effects of bereavement.

Unless legal or financial circumstances dictate immediate action on some issue, you should avoid making key decisions until you have overcome the symptoms of grief and you've found the friends and professionals who can provide you with sound advice. Take your time and don't let anyone force you to make a decision—to sell the family home, for instance—until you have regained your emotional equilibrium and found a new support group. And as I suggested earlier, you may very well need help from a qualified therapist to determine when you've reached that point.

Once you achieve a new equilibrium, you must carefully consider the strengths and weaknesses of the personal and professional advice you receive. And then make your key decisions. If you've made your best effort to consider the opinions of friends and experts concerning, for example, the sale of an asset, all you can do is hope you got the balance right. Six months later, whether you decided to keep or sell the asset, if you can sleep at night, you probably made the right decision. However, if you feel you made the wrong decision, don't fall into a trough of guilt or depression. You have just faced some of the most trying and difficult decisions of your entire life. Cut yourself some slack and pat yourself on the back for all the good decisions you made.

To summarize all my warnings so far, keep this rule in mind when trying to distinguish and balance personal and professional advice, and you'll have a much better chance of managing your inheritance successfully: Don't treat a trusted friend as an expert or a trusted expert as a friend.

I'm sorry to say I can't tell you how to find good friends. But, as a lawyer and entrepreneur, I can tell you a few things about how to find good professionals. The first problem you face when trying to find a good professional is, generally, you can't go to a professional to get an honest appraisal of other professionals, for a couple of reasons. Professional bodies, especially in medicine and law, prevent their members from criticizing one another because a peer's membership in the professional fraternity in itself is supposed to vouch for his or her competence. If an expert wishes to criticize a peer, the body generally demands evidence of misconduct so severe that it requires professional disciplinary action. An expert will also avoid criticizing a peer for fear of inciting an escalating war of criticism that could damage the critic as much as the person criticized. The critic may also fear a defamation suit. So, unless you already know a good expert in a field who is willing to steer you in the direction of other competent colleagues and away from the incompetent, you can't rely on experts themselves to send you to the right experts.

Obviously, taking referrals from friends who've had positive experiences with certain professionals is a traditional and often effective way to find good advice. However, we run into the same problem here that we ran into earlier concerning friendly advice. Just as a friend's opinions may not be suited to your values, life style and experiences, so too, your friends' experts may not be suited to them. Although the expert to whom you were referred is extremely competent, you may find the two of you just don't have the chemistry needed to develop a trusting and effective relationship.

The first step in evaluating any expert is to realize that the expert doesn't simply represent you, the client. He has other interests to represent when providing advice, and some of them point away from providing you with the best possible service. Every expert who works with colleagues in a firm environment has at least three separate interests to consider. The first is his self-interest in persuading you to use his services. The second is the firm's interest, which the expert must promote if he hopes to move up within the firm and increase his share of its revenue. The third is your interest in receiving the best possible advice.

In an ideal world, your interest should come first; the expert's self-interest and the firm's interest should come a distant second. In the real world, however, the latter interests often come first. The expert has to keep a steady stream of clients moving through the firm to keep his billings up and impress his partners. This means that he has a monetary and career interest in persuading you to use his services, even if he and his colleagues don't have much experience in dealing with problems like yours. To score points with the partners, he also has an interest in referring you to other firm members for additional services, even though they may not be the most competent professionals he knows.

On the other hand, if he refers you to someone outside the firm, don't take that as a sure sign he's selflessly sending you to the best expert to deal with your problems. He may owe a referral to someone who gave him a referral in the past; he may want to help a former schoolmate who needs the business; or, if he refers you to someone in another field—for example, your lawyer refers you to an accountant—he simply may be honoring a reciprocal referral agreement. The reasons for self-interested referrals are endless. Only you can be sure that your interests remain paramount. How do you do that? In what follows, I want to offer some tips on how to make sure an expert will be looking out for your interests.

I'll begin with the questions you should put to a lawyer because that's the profession I know best. However, these questions should also be addressed to any professional who's working in a firm environment.

## Lawyers

I begin here by proposing something that most non-experts will find daunting: Interview a lawyer before you agree to retain him or her. Most people are intimidated by the notion of questioning someone who is trained in the art of examination. However, only by investigating the expert and his or her practice can you come to an informed decision about whether to use him or her.

Before you commit yourself to anyone, ask for some free time (15 minutes to a half-hour) for an interview. When you meet with a lawyer, begin by asking whether he has experience with your kind of estate problems and assets. Find out how many years he's been working with clients on these matters and what percentage of his work is still devoted to them. Ask him up front whether your bequest is too large or too small for him to deal with. Ask what he bills, how he bills (by the hour or by transaction or both) and let him know honestly whether you can afford him. Ask whether he will personally do the work or whether he'll simply turn it over to juniors. (Turning your file over to juniors is fine, as long as they have the right experience and your lawyer guarantees that he will supervise them. It might save you a lot of money in the end since juniors will be billed at lower rates.) Ask him whether he is planning to move up in the organization and away from clients with your profile in the near future. If he is planning to move up soon, ask how your file will be dealt with during the transition period.

Another technique is to present some hypothetical problems that are similar to the ones you're facing, or simply choose one of your problems and ask each interviewee how he would deal with it. Keep notes and compare answers. Some will look better than others. How the advice is delivered (i.e., whether it is clear and respectful of your level of understanding) will also tell you whether you can work with this person. You should expect to receive all your answers in plain English—if he uses too much jargon and won't explain what it means clearly, don't use him.

Once you've chosen a lawyer, you should monitor his performance to ensure you've made the right choice. Make sure he responds to your letters and calls promptly. (Law societies and bar associations set strict guidelines for timely responses; you can find out what they are by calling your local society or association.) Be sure that your lawyer's recommendations are implemented and administered efficiently.

You can assess the firm's performance by calling a junior, assistant or secretary to check on the status of your file. Has that key letter been mailed out? Have all probate forms and affidavits been submitted to the court? Have documents relating to a real estate transaction been drafted and sent out to all parties? A lawyer may give excellent advice; however, if his firm is poorly administered by the support staff, that advice will be for naught. Poor administration is a sign that you should be taking your business elsewhere. Don't be afraid to make calls and ask those questions when circumstances indicate that something wasn't said, written or sent on time or in the proper way.

One of the greatest myths of using a lawyer, or any professional, is that you can sit back and let him or her take care of everything. A professional's advice is effective only if it reflects a clear understanding of your situation and wishes. As protection against client-lawyer misunderstandings, one of my former colleagues carefully listens to a new client's complaints and then asks, "So, what do you want me to do?" Sometimes the client knows, sometimes he doesn't. In either case, this attorney learns very quickly whether his client has a clear understanding of what he needs or wants from his lawyer and the litigation process.

Not every lawyer will size up a client as well as my friend does. That means the burden is on you to explain to your lawyer what you hope to achieve by using his services. It also means that you must double-check your lawyer's work to ensure that he fully understands and protects your interests at all times. Read every key document he writes, uses or receives (ask for copies), and when the paperwork isn't flowing smoothly, by all means, call and ask questions.

Also, don't forget (and I'm sure you won't) to measure your lawyer's performance against his billings. If you don't understand how your lawyer calculated his billing, ask him to itemize his services; if he's billing on an hourly rather than transactional basis, ask for a breakdown of time spent on key matters. Most lawyers will provide these details as a matter of course, but if your lawyer doesn't, again, don't be afraid to ask. If he's reluctant to itemize his charges, consider finding another attorney.

Aside from these questions, which, as I said previously, should be addressed to any professional working in a firm or partnership, in what follows, I'll give you some specific tips on how to evaluate professionals in other fields.

## Stockbrokers

In addition to all the general questions listed previously, when you interview a broker, ask her to describe the three biggest losses she ever suffered and the three biggest gains she ever realized and what she learned from them. Ask her for a sample portfolio that displays results over a period of years. Be sure to find out what her areas of specialization are. If she's the firm's oil and gas expert, you're going to see quite a few proposals for natural resource stocks, even if the market is performing poorly in those areas. She'll have to flog these products for the firm regardless of whether they're the best investments for you. You can't trust her to give completely unbiased advice concerning your investment options. So you really have to know beforehand which areas you want to pursue.

Since the world of stocks can be difficult to understand, try to find someone who is willing to teach you how, where and why she wants to invest your money. If you're stuck with someone who simply dictates an investment strategy, look for another broker.

Also, ask whether the firm does its own research or buys it from other sources. Ultimately, risks are hedged by knowing more than the other guy about the present and future health of a company. The broker who has the best research is going to keep you one step ahead of the pack. Be careful of brokers who buy their information from other firms or independent analysts. This is a sure sign that your advantage has been lost. Other firms will get the information to their clients first and independent analysts will sell their reports to other brokers. As a result, competing investors will have access to the same "exclusive" information you do.

Again, I stress the need to monitor the actions of your expert. Never give your broker the written authority to trade without your consent. You can never tell what may happen.

# Trust Company Executives

Acting as the manager of someone else's wealth is a noble calling and many trust companies have attracted able, high-minded administrators. However, in some companies, the trust executive sits pretty low on the food chain of financial advisors. He is like a soft-shell bottom-feeder. He's not very aggressive, creative or innovative and isn't expected to be. He just sits there and waits for someone to die and place some assets in his custody. His charge comes from a will that gives him the right to manage the inheritance of a beneficiary. He didn't earn his position by proving his business acumen to your benefactor. In fact, quite the opposite. He was appointed to give you the stodgiest and thus the safest possible management of your inheritance. His role is merely to preserve your wealth, not to enhance it.

The limits of the trust executive's authority are contained in your benefactor's will and various statutes. In some cases, they leave the trust executive with very little leeway to manage your bequest. He can be limited to a narrow range of very safe investments, such as bonds and residential mortgages. (Even when the will and legislation give him a free hand, his strategy will tend to be very cautious for reasons we'll consider in a moment.)

Your benefactor believed that this would be a great arrangement. He could leave his money with someone who will make sure you don't blow it on Ferraris or trips to Vegas. The beneficiary may like it as well. He can carry on with his life without worrying about how to manage his wealth.

However, the virtue of the trust executive—his inherent conservatism—is also his vice. In both Canada and the United States, the trustee's complacency is sometimes assured by the fact that certain jurisdictions make it very difficult to replace him and so he is never penalized for poor performance. To make matters worse, in many states a corporate trustee has the freedom to raise management fees at regular intervals. Even in states where fees are limited by statute, the trustee often has a lot of room to jack up the rates. This, of course, means that he can continually mismanage assets with impunity. And if you decide to sue him for losses incurred by his negligence, think again. His legal fees are paid by the trust, a fact that often discourages beneficiaries from pursuing legitimate claims.

All this means that some corporate trustees provide nothing more and sometimes something less than safe management.

It's worth noting that a nonprofit organization called Heirs is trying to resolve these problems by lobbying the Pennsylvania legislature to pass a law that would give dissatisfied beneficiaries the right to replace a corporate trustee with another of their choosing. Heirs believes that the threat of replacement would force apathetic trustees to provide a higher level of service and performance. And, no doubt, it would.

For the foregoing reasons, plus the fact that trust administration sometimes doesn't attract those who have ambition, ideas or exceptional talent, you cannot be relieved of the task of managing your inheritance. To protect yourself from an incompetent or indifferent trustee, you must oversee and second-guess everything he recommends and does. In the best case, you should use lawyers, accountants and financial advisors to evaluate your trustee's proposals. You should also use them to develop a more effective investment strategy that can be used to prod your trustee into producing a better investment plan.

Also, be on guard at all times against the possibility that your trustee may try to advise on matters that exceed his jurisdiction and expertise. One of the damning aspects of trust legislation in certain jurisdictions is that it limits the liabilities of a trustee to the areas over which he exercises his very limited jurisdiction. This means he isn't liable if he gives you negligent advice on an issue that isn't within the scope of his authority. In many states and provinces, for example, he isn't empowered to give tax advice. Yet if he decides to give you tax advice, you rely on it, and it turns out to be wrong, that's your problem, not his. To avoid this situation, be sure to consult your lawyer to determine the exact scope of your trustee's authority and don't let him exceed it. As in our example, if he gives tax advice, don't let him charge for it, don't rely on it, and review his recommendations with a tax lawyer and an accountant.

To summarize, when you are left with a trustee to monitor and manage your inheritance, you must use other professionals to monitor and manage your trustee.

## Art/Antique Experts

This is a field that is not governed by special statutes, a professional body or a code of ethics, and it doesn't require a high level of education or a specialist's degree. Some people at major auction houses may hold degrees in art or art history, but that isn't the norm for the art/antique world as a whole. As one jaded auction expert with a famous international firm once said to me, "There are false specialists everywhere; what they don't know, they make up." The snobbery of the art expert may be a pose designed to cover up his or her lack of training and sophistication.

The problem in dealing with most art or antique experts is that they can deceitfully mix personal advice, expert advice and self-interest. An expert may give you an accurate report on the quality and provenance of an object (maybe you've got an authentic Art Deco vase from your mother's estate) and then give you some personal advice. He might criticize its style, suggest it's not tasteful, or convince you that it doesn't suit your life style, to persuade you to let him buy it or sell it. If he really wants the piece, he might also provide an unduly low estimate of its value to make you think it's not worth keeping, or encourage a sale by convincing you that the market is "hot." You can be sure an art expert is up to no good when he wants you to make a snap decision to sell. If you're not sure whether to dissolve an object, just remember that it can always be stored until you decide what to do with it. (In the case of precious or fragile objects, store these only with moving or storage companies that have low-traffic, high-security premises devoted to antiques and art.)

Generally, your choice of experts should be determined by your feeling about the potential value of an object. If you want to evaluate and sell an object that may have international importance, such as an Impressionist painting, a 19th-century Persian carpet or an 18th-century sterling silver tea service, use the services of an auction house that has an international presence. Christie's and Sotheby's are obvious choices. For valuable but less significant objects, such as antique North American furniture or modern sterling silver flatware, use a strong regional auction house that draws clients from a number of urban centers. For anything else, from washing machines to contemporary dining-room sets, consider the auctioneers whose focus is local, unless the regional houses have an interest in these items.

In all cases, whether you're dealing with precious or mundane objects, you must get competing estimates from different auctioneers and evaluators. Some auction houses can achieve much higher returns than others with the same objects because they have access to collectors and dealers who specialize in those objects. Also, some houses have good evaluators and some don't. An incompetent evaluator might easily miss the value of that small Oriental throw rug in your grandmother's den. He might think it's worth $500 while the carpet specialist from a competitor will realize that it's worth $15,000. If you suspect that any object has significant value, you should get three independent evaluations. You may have to pay evaluators' fees, which generally aren't oppressive, if you use an auctioneer and don't choose to consign any objects to him. But just remember that the cost of undervaluing and underselling objects may be much greater than the fees you expend to get competing evaluations.

Once you have established the real value of your inherited possessions, you must decide whether to keep or sell them. Chapter 7 will deal with all the moral and psychological problems involved in making those decisions. If we assume for a moment that you've decided to sell, you should consider three alternatives.

You can of course sell your possessions at auction. Auctions allow you to realize a fast buck on a possession, but keep in mind, in most cases, that you'll receive only half the "market" value of the object. (Half the "market" value equals the "auction" value.) That's true for a couple of reasons. First, at least half the bidders at an auction are dealers who will pay only half the market value of any object that they would sell in their stores (wholesale-to-retail markup is almost always 100 percent). Second, the other bidders are collectors who are looking for a good deal. Sometimes serious collectors may make bids that far exceed an object's auction value, and even its market value, but don't count on it. The multimillion dollar competition for paintings at Christie's and Sotheby's is the exception, not the rule.

On the business side, be sure that you negotiate commissions and moving charges with an auction company. Commissions vary depending on the value of an object and may range anywhere from 20 percent for less valuable items to 10 percent for the more valuable. If you consign a number of objects, or a few objects of outstanding worth, keep in mind that the auctioneer may consider lowering his commissions or writing off some or all of his moving charges to get your business. To get a discount on fees, let auctioneer A know that auctioneer B will cut you a better deal if A won't give you the same deal or a better one. And be sure when you finally do strike a deal, that *all* the terms are embodied in a written contract. Remember, unless you have a separate written agreement concerning commissions and charges, the standard terms of sale that are listed in the auction catalog will be binding on buyer and seller. In the absence of written variations, those terms will allow the auctioneer to take his standard commission, regardless of what may have been said during your phone conversation the week before the sale.

The written agreement can also give you another very important piece of protection that you must insist on: reserve prices. A reserve is the price below which you refuse to allow the auctioneer to sell your possession. If, for instance, you receive an auction estimate of $4,000 to $5,000 for your grandmother's piano, but you wouldn't want to part with it for anything less than $3,000, specify in the contract that the auctioneer cannot accept a bid of less than $3,000. If he does, he'll be liable for the difference between the sale and reserve prices. Generally, a reserve will be set at 10 to 20 percent less than the low-end auction estimate; however, that shouldn't stop you from insisting on a higher reserve figure if that's what you want.

And just to keep your auctioneer honest, be sure to prepare your own itemized list of consigned items in advance of moving day. You can use your list to check against the catalog to ensure that every item actually made it to the floor and wasn't purchased by someone else for a bargain price before the actual sale. Better yet, visit the auction floor before the sale and check to see that every item on your list is on the floor, in the catalog and priced according to the auction estimate (for example, $4,000 to $5,000 for grandmother's piano).

## Real Estate Agents

The first way to weed out the good from the bad in this field is to refuse to deal with anyone who pursues your business aggressively immediately after a bereavement. If you've inherited residential real estate, some agents show up at your home with unseemly haste. In my own case, 48 hours after my mother died, a neighbor showed up at our family home with his girlfriend, who was a real estate agent, and demanded an immediate tour of the home so they could be the first in line to buy or sell. I might have excused his behavior since he had alcohol on his breath, but his friend, the agent, didn't. Anyone who tries to pressure you into selling property in the first days or weeks after a bereavement is trying to take advantage of your weakness. Strike that kind of agent off your list from the start.

Here's someone else you might consider striking off your list: a broker's top seller. Don't hire him believing that he will get you the best price for your property. The top seller is at the top not because he gets the highest prices for properties but because he's an expert at playing sellers and buyers off against one another to achieve the quickest possible sale. He may very well try to persuade you to sell low so he can get his commission and move on to the next sale.

Should you eventually decide to sell your residential property, your first step is to get at least two independent evaluations of the property from qualified members of a certified appraisal institute. You can get a list of qualified appraisers from your local real estate board. If possible, find out from your local banker which appraiser he uses to evaluate properties for mortgage purposes. Any appraiser who has earned the trust of a banker will probably give you an honest, conservative estimate of the value of your property.

Once you know what your property is really worth, you can weed out good agents from bad according to the accuracy of their own estimates. An agent who overvalues your property is trying to appeal to your greed to persuade you to list with him. Once you've listed, two months later he will ask you to drastically drop the price because he's "surprised" that the market isn't performing well at the moment. An agent who undervalues your property wants you to sell to one of his friends or clients at a bargain price. You may find that the appraiser, if he's also an agent, is the best person, in the end, to represent your property.

When you finally decide to sign a listing agreement with someone, be sure that you limit the listing to 30 to 60 days, and renew only if you feel your agent is making his best efforts. An agent will try to persuade you to list for at least 90 days, which is a long time if you've chosen the wrong agent.

Another test for your agent is his conduct when he brings you an offer sheet. To get his commission quickly, he may try to persuade you to take a low offer. If he's really desperate or crooked, he and the offering agent may meet with you and encourage you to sign the sheet. If your agent pressures you to take an offer, fire him on the spot. Your agent is *your* agent; he's there to communicate your wishes to other parties, not to impose his own on you. To ensure that this situation doesn't arise, discuss the offer with your agent only after you've discussed it with your lawyer. He will keep you sensitive to the conflicts of interest that some agents bring to the bargaining table.

## Bankers

A bank makes its biggest returns from interest charges on loans, especially loans that come in the form of outstanding credit card balances, which can attract rates as high as 18 percent. So be assured that a banker's primary purpose will be to sell you debt. As soon as your bank account reflects a tidy inheritance, your banker will be calling to let you know that you have the power to borrow against cash and other assets. Due to deregulation, which has allowed banks to broaden the range of their services, a banker's second purpose will be to sell you products: mutual funds, Treasury bills, government bonds, corporate debentures and bank-issued securities. He or she may also suggest setting up a tax-sheltered retirement fund, buying and selling stocks without a broker on a computerized trading system or opening a foreign currency account. You'll be told that you shouldn't leave your cash in a savings account where lower interest rates may not outstrip the rate of inflation; if you want real security, better to invest immediately in a bank product that promises a significant return.

It's pretty hard to go wrong with T-bills, U.S. or Canadian government bonds, or bank-issued securities (assuming your bank is well-managed); however, other products will involve higher levels of risk. To properly evaluate the risk, you will need the advice of other professionals, especially a reliable stockbroker if you plan to invest in foreign currencies or trade stocks and mutual funds. You should also seek the advice of an accountant to measure the value of your potential investment against tax consequences accruing from interest income and capital gains.

Keep in mind that a loan, even one that is small relative to your net worth, can entail serious risk if it isn't linked to a comprehensive financial plan. You and your banker can easily convince yourselves that a loan is a safe and suitable investment in a car, a home or a business venture because safety and suitability are defined on a very narrow basis. You qualify for a loan as long as your net worth statement, a bank form you must complete, discloses hard capital assets (such as cash, property, vehicles, stocks or bonds) that exceed the value of your debt and that can be pledged as security. In other words, as long as the bank can be paid back, your banker is satisfied that taking on debt was the right thing for you to do. But was it?

Your net worth statement doesn't tell you or your banker anything about whether your loan was suited to your future needs and goals. Let me illustrate how that fact can destroy an inheritance with a brief case study of a young woman from Raleigh, North Carolina.

Lorraine was the favorite niece of Joe, her mother's only sibling who was a highly successfully independent insurance agent from New Hampshire. When Joe, who was single, had a fatal heart attack at the age of 50, Lorraine, who had just turned 30, found herself the beneficiary of a $150,000 insurance policy and a summer cottage in Maine worth about $175,000.

When her bank discovered that she had deposited the proceeds of the policy in her savings account, an account manager, Christine, called to encourage her to meet to discuss ways of investing the cash. Lorraine, a public school teacher with little financial experience, was looking for advice and was grateful for the call. When they met, Christine learned that Lorraine wanted to sell the cottage in Maine and buy a $175,000 condominium in Raleigh because she had always heard that urban property was the best long-term investment. Christine proposed that Lorraine make a $50,000 down payment on the condo and use the remaining $100,000 in cash, as well as the cottage, to leverage a $125,000 loan that would be paid down from the eventual sale of the Maine property.

A year later, Lorraine's plans had changed and her condo purchase became a nightmare. She took the loan as a line of credit, which meant that the interest rate varied with the prime. When the prime shot up due to sharp increases in the rate of inflation, her bank payments began to exceed her disposable income. Then she delayed the sale of the cottage when she learned from a family friend that her uncle had hoped she would keep the cottage in the family. Her long-term career goals also shifted after a colleague suggested using her inheritance to earn a graduate degree in education, which would greatly improve her income earning power, would be a better long-term investment than a condominium.

After deciding that she should honor her uncle's wishes and keep the cottage, she tried to sell the condo. However, a hike in interest rates and a temporary glut in the condo market depressed the value of her property and made it difficult to unload. She eventually faced a power of sale for failure to meet her bank payments and parted with the condo for $85,000. The bank took the entire $100,000 from her savings account and $30,000 from the proceeds of the sale to cover the loan and sale-related expenses. Lorraine was left with $55,000, which she soon discovered was needed to meet yearly taxes and maintenance expenses on the cottage. Her dream of a better career went out the window with her cash.

Lorraine needed time for reflection as well as financial and career counseling before making the decision to buy a condominium. She shouldn't have expected to get counseling from her banker, who simply wasn't qualified to give it.

As the advertising suggests, your friendly neighborhood banker is most likely a very decent, well-trained person who wants to help you to create wealth, not waste it. Unfortunately, his limited knowledge of your affairs can make him complicitous in a financial disaster. To avoid that end, carefully analyze your short-term needs and goals with the assistance of other experts, such as your accountant, lawyer and broker, before buying bank products or borrowing funds.

Let me make a few random points about dealing with bankers before we leave this section. First, if you ever find yourself with a debt that has spiraled out of control, as Lorraine's had, remember that a banker would always prefer to save you than sink you. (A high default ratio, even if losses are small, means no promotion.) If you're facing default, the best strategy is to see your banker as soon as trouble is on the horizon, disclose your problem, present a plan for solving it and bargain for temporary relief, such as a short-term suspension of principal payments. Notice and honesty help you and your banker. Notice gives him time to examine alternatives to default and honesty gives him reason to believe that he can trust you to carry out an alternative payment plan.

Another point: A banker loves a net worth statement because it gives him a license to sell products and float loans. This means he'll do everything possible to get you to disclose the full extent of your inheritance. I would advise against doing this for two reasons. First, while he promises confidentiality, your statement will be seen by many people in the banking system, some of whom may not be as tight-lipped as your key contact. Second, you really need to declare only the minimal amount that is needed to support the security needs of a specific transaction. If a declaration of $100,000 in assets is all you need to get that $50,000 business loan, don't volunteer additional information. To determine what you must declare, just ask your banker to specify the minimum amount that would have to be pledged for any particular transaction, then declare only what he needs. If he refuses to specify the asset-to-transaction ratio, explain how disappointed you would be if you had to offer your business to another bank. The basic rule of thumb for net worth statements is *maintain your privacy*; *declare as little as possible.* (Full disclosure is warranted only if your banker is also your financial planner.)

Also, remember that banks are always competing for business. To get yours, a bank may be willing to waive standard bank charges for processing transactions, from the most basic, such as check returns, to the most complex. Don't be afraid to bargain.

Finally, when considering any transaction, be sure to read all the documents that your banker asks you to sign. Since banking institutions present an image of trust and banking forms are long and poorly written, clients have a tendency to sign whatever is put in front of them. To avoid binding yourself to more obligations than you want or need, ask for copies of the forms before meeting with your banker to finalize a transaction, review them in detail, ask him to explain any terms you can't understand and be sure to have them reviewed by your lawyer.

## Accountants

I offer three warnings to guide you in dealing with accountants: First, don't assume that every accountant understands all the ins and outs of dealing with estate matters. In large urban areas where specialization is the norm, many accountants will not have practiced actively in the area. If you interview someone who doesn't have a lot of experience with estates, he or she should refer you to a colleague who has an estates practice. To be sure that the colleague does, ask him whether he deals with estate issues on a regular basis. If he doesn't, kindly ask him to refer you to someone who does.

My second warning is: Don't assume that your accountant can give you good business advice. Many clients mistakenly believe that because an accountant can give them advice on how to organize their assets to avoid taxes, she also knows a great deal about how to run a business or make a solid investment. The fact that someone knows how to apply the arcane provisions of the tax code is no guarantee that she has good business judgment. That comes only from playing the role of businessperson or investor. If your accountant has played those roles, she might in fact give you sound advice concerning the management or investment of an inheritance. However, if she isn't an experienced businessperson, her advice might prove to be no more useful than the tip you received from your mail carrier. If your accountant offers business advice, be sure to discuss it with your other advisers before acting on it.

Finally, be careful about relying exclusively on your accountant for advice concerning the tax issues involved in managing a large or complicated estate. In my experience, such an estate can produce accounting and legal problems that are often intertwined. To ensure that the accounting advice gives you the maximum tax protection the law can provide, have a competent estate lawyer or a tax lawyer with estate experience review the recommendations of your accountant. Instruct your accountant to send copies of her recommendations to your attorney before acting on her advice.

# Chapter 6

# Family Conflicts

So far, we have been considering the grieving inheritor primarily in relation to the deceased or the inheritance. In Chapters 2 and 3, we examined how an inheritor's reaction to the loss of a loved one can give rise to attitudes that interfere with the management of an inheritance. In Chapter 4, we examined how an inheritor's reaction to the inheritance itself can give rise to other harmful attitudes. In Chapter 5, we considered how to find advisers who can help you to avoid these attitudes and make sound financial judgments. In this chapter, I examine how an inheritance can interfere with family relationships. In particular, I focus on relationships among siblings since they are the source of the most common and embittering forms of family conflict following a bereavement.

In describing the general causes of sibling conflict, I begin with the concept of equilibrium.[1] A favorite of family therapists, it expresses a relatively simple idea. To satisfy its basic needs, every family must call upon its members to play various roles. When roles satisfy needs, the family achieves a state of balance or equilibrium, which is characterized by the absence of serious conflict. This state, however, is difficult to maintain because the needs of some members will change over time. Unless other members change their roles in response,[2] needs will be frustrated and conflict can emerge.

We can use this concept to pinpoint three basic causes of sibling conflict. The first cause is something called "role substitution." When a parent dies, sometimes a sibling, often the eldest, will assume the parent's role. If the parent exercised an important leadership role,[3] someone will certainly be needed to perform some of the parent's functions while the family finds a new way to organize itself. However, if the sibling who takes the helm doesn't have leadership skills, the family can break up on the shoals of misunderstanding, resentment and jealousy.[4]

The sibling who imposes his leadership may have begun his run on his parent's position long before the death. If the parent was terminally ill or infirm, the sibling might have asserted dominion by making important medical or financial decisions without consulting his brothers and sisters. In itself, that can lead to resentment long after the parent is gone, especially if the decisions hastened death or precipitated financial loss. That same sibling might also seek to control funeral arrangements and important estate matters. This situation is made much worse if other siblings are contending for the role of substitute parent. Then resentments double, and often therapists and lawyers are needed to open lines of communication and resolve conflicts.

The second cause of sibling conflict arises when the deceased parent was a mediator who took the lead in resolving sibling conflicts or was an iron-fisted tyrant who suppressed all differences. In either case, sibling rivalries are left free to flourish, often with devastating results. Lois Akner describes this problem with great clarity:

> When a parent dies, the adult children can be forced to confront the truth about family relationships. Any ambivalence you may have felt toward one another is brought to the fore, and a lifetime of hidden resentments and regrets are ripped open to create fresh wounds.[5]

Conflicts can also emerge because the children previously submerged their differences out of loyalty to a parent, regardless of whether he or she played a significant leadership role in the family.

The third cause of conflict resides in the simple fact that siblings have something new over which to fight. For years, they may have been leading separate lives. Yet now they are forced to consider in common how an estate should be administered. In cases where a will leaves assets to the children collectively, they must also consider how to distribute wealth. In the latter case, siblings can regress and behave like children battling over how much dessert each should get or who should share his toys with the others.

Three additional causes of sibling conflict can be found in the way that family members express their grief.

First, if the family is uncomfortable with open and direct expressions of grief, the symptoms of each family member will manifest themselves indirectly. This can produce conflict in various ways. If, for example, a family suppresses its anger, siblings may take it out on another sibling who becomes a scapegoat for the family's financial and emotional turmoils.[6] The sibling who was most often picked on as a child might endure censure because "he said or did the wrong thing," which then is treated as a primary cause of family discord and unhappiness. In the same way, the sibling who made key medical decisions for a dying parent might be forced to shoulder the blame for the death: "If only Margaret had forced Dad to consider trying chemotherapy before undergoing surgery, he would probably still be with us today."

The second grief-related cause of sibling conflict is rooted in the fact that family members often do not understand that they might express their grief in different ways.[7] One of the first families I ever represented suffered from this problem. I was invited to the family home the day after the father, who had been diagnosed with Alzheimer's disease, had committed suicide. He left a note stating that he had decided to take his own life so he and his family wouldn't have to suffer through his inevitable decline. When the eldest son, Josh, greeted me at the door, he was collected and jovial, as if nothing had happened. We retired to the living room where Josh expressed relief and joy about his father's death. He saw the suicide as an act of courage that deserved to be celebrated. In stark contrast, his younger brother Larry, who soon joined us, couldn't stop sobbing. After the first 10 minutes of our meeting, Larry became enraged, blurted out that Josh must have hated their father, and stormed out of the room. In fact, Josh had loved his father dearly but couldn't bring himself to mourn immediately. It took about three weeks for his grief to come to the surface. One day, when he was driving home from work, quite unexpectedly, the tears began to flow.

As many siblings do, Josh and Larry expressed their grief in different ways and at different times. Larry, though, didn't immediately understand this fact and held a grudge against Josh for smiling and laughing the day after their father's death. This led Larry to adopt a confrontational stance in his dealings with Josh, which proved to be the cause of many unnecessary and unpleasant conflicts in the ensuing months.

The final cause of grief-related conflict is the heightened sensitivities that result from experiencing grief. Family members, regardless of how they express their grief, experience a high level of stress in the days following their bereavement. Everyone is irritable and easily offended. As a result, personalities clash more easily and small differences can become major rifts.[8]

When any of the aforementioned conflicts exist, they often produce secondary conflicts over the inheritance in the following situations: 1) when a sibling is appointed sole executor, especially if he or she exercises authority arbitrarily or with too much vigour; 2) when bequests are distributed unequally; and 3) when the will empowers the executor to distribute personal possessions at his or her discretion or it leaves the siblings to determine the distribution among themselves. I now examine each of these situations in detail.

# 1. The Heavy-Handed Executor

A parent might have decided to give the role of executor to one sibling for any number of reasons. Perhaps he or she was the only sibling who lived in the parent's vicinity; maybe family tradition dictated that the eldest should supervise the family's financial affairs; or one sibling might have professional expertise in financial or legal matters. However simple or expedient the reason may have been, giving the executorship to one sibling is often perceived by other siblings as an act of parental favoritism; as such, it can ignite old rivalries and conflicts.

This problem is exacerbated if the executor takes his appointment as a sign that he is now the head of the family. That can lead him to abuse his authority or, at the least, exercise it in a heavy-handed manner that is perceived as abusive. The intensity of the resulting conflict will depend on how much discretion is left to the executor by the terms of the will. Does he have complete control of assets requiring ongoing management, such as a family business? Does he have discretionary control over the distribution of personal possessions? Does he have the discretionary power to dissolve or retain principal assets? If he has any or all of these powers, he has the means of impressing his will on his siblings. Should he fail to consult them on important matters that are within his discretion, he will provoke a hostile reaction. The way in which a sibling executor can abuse his authority is illustrated by our next case study.

Horace and Myra Zeffer were always very generous with their four children—John, Barry, Jenny and Marie. Horace had been a successful corporate executive with a national electronics firm based in Eugene, Oregon. He had used his substantial income to ensure that his children received good educations and that they had enough money to get a start in life. When Horace died suddenly at the age of 59, Myra, who had been a devoted wife and mother and a lifelong member of several charitable organizations, continued to give liberally to her children. This was facilitated by her considerable inheritance, which included her husband's stock portfolio and his corporate pension benefits.

Examples of the Zeffers' benefactions were numerous. They put Jenny through a college humanities program, bought her a car as a graduation present, picked up the tab for her year at teacher's college and gave her financial assistance until she found her first teaching job. Marie, who didn't go to college and married in her early twenties, was given a sizable down payment on her family's first home. The Zeffers also paid for John's college education and his postgraduate degree in business. Although Barry didn't attend college, his parents funded years of private training in music. And when he decided to launch a career as a music teacher, they invested in his first studio.

The Zeffers' generosity was also reflected in the way they shared their vacation property with their children. The five-acre site, overlooking a small lake, had been purchased by Horace 25 years earlier as a summer and weekend hideaway. On it was a large family cottage, to which Mrs. Zeffer had retired after her husband's death, and a small rental cottage. Over the years, the Zeffers made sure that every child had his or her own place on the property. When Jenny turned 30, she was given the rental cottage. John had been allowed to build his own cottage on a large one-acre site. Barry, who couldn't afford to build his own cottage, was given a substantial sum to build his own place; he was left with a small mortgage, amounting to about 40 percent of the dwelling's value, which Myra paid off over a period of several years. Marie and her family, who lived in Texas, didn't really need their own cottage because they visited the retreat only once a year. Horace and Myra had always allowed them to stay in the family cottage.

When Myra Zeffer died, she left a will that stipulated strict equality in the division of her liquid assets. She left $50,000 to each of her children with the remainder divided equally among her grandchildren. The family property, which was still in Myra's name, was divided equally among the children, each receiving one and one-quarter acres with a cottage on each parcel. The exception to the rule of equality was Marie's bequest. She was given the family cottage, which was by far the largest and most valuable dwelling. However, everyone recognized that she had received less than the others in the past because she had never drawn on family money to attend college or pursue vocational training. The transfer of the largest cottage more or less settled the score in the minds of her siblings.

John, however, had a problem with the distribution of property to Jenny and Barry. He was aggrieved because their cottages had been given to them while he had paid for his. The only way to redress this inequality, he felt, was to compel Jenny and Barry to pay the estate for the right to hold on to their cottages. While John couldn't find a way to force Jenny to pay for her cottage since it had been given to her outright, he did see a way of forcing Barry to pay for his. As executor, John had access to the checks (now canceled) that had been written by his mother to cover the mortgage on Barry's cottage. He produced them as evidence that Barry had owed his mother, and now owed her estate, close to $40,000. That put Barry in a terrible bind. Since he couldn't afford to re-mortgage the cottage, he would have to sell it to satisfy the debt.

John felt free to impose his own view of economic justice on the family because, as sole executor and the eldest, he saw himself as the new head of the family. And he was upfront about it. When meeting with Barry to discuss the debt, John clearly explained why he felt an inequality existed and insisted that he had the right to redress it. He was not explicit, though, about his other motive. John had always been secretly resentful of Barry. Hard-nosed and practical since boyhood, John had never respected his parents' decision to spend so much money on Barry's musical education when a musical career promised so little in the way of financial return. In this respect, he felt that Barry had received special treatment. John's resentment was reinforced by his perception that Barry had been his mother's favorite son. Myra had always seemed to take a special relish in Barry's accomplishments because, as she was so fond of saying, "Barry got his musical talents from my side of the family."

Barry's response to John's insistence on the existence of the debt was also rooted in sibling history. He felt that his older brother was playing the bully and beating up on him just as he had when they were younger. This time, he resolved, he wouldn't allow himself to be pushed around. He didn't appeal to the estate's solicitor to resolve the problem. Instead, he hired his own lawyer, who threatened litigation if John attempted to enforce a claim on behalf of the estate. Barry's lawyer argued that, given Myra's history of gift-giving, and the absence of any document or letter of understanding referring to these payments as loans, Myra's payments would have to be regarded as gifts. Reluctantly, John accepted Barry's position after consulting the estate's lawyer, who confirmed the validity of the opposing counsel's argument.

Using the basic facts of our case study, we can also imagine one other possible cause of conflict resulting from role substitution. Assume for a moment that instead of coveting the role of executor, John saw it as an annoying encroachment on the time and energy he needed to devote to his demanding corporate job. In turn, he became resentful of his siblings because they were not forced to make any sacrifices to administer the estate. We could see his claim against Barry as a way of equalizing the burden of managing the estate.

This conflict could also have arisen from differences resulting from the way in which the family members grieved. Imagine, for a moment, that John and Barry went to war because of hindrances to the expression of grief within the family. Let's assume that John could not openly express his anger for failing "somehow" to prevent his mother's death. As a result, he expressed it indirectly by blaming Barry for ignoring warning signs of ill health. In this instance, we could see the claim against Barry as a symptom of John's grief rather than a symptom of disequilibrium.

We could also attribute this conflict to another problem resulting from differences in grieving. Let's assume that John was overwhelmed by his loss and openly expressed his grief while Barry got stuck in denial and didn't immediately manifest symptoms such as pining and sorrow. John took Barry's delayed reaction as a sign that he cared less for his mother than he should have or that he was callously ignoring his brother's feelings. In either case, John's claim against Barry might then be interpreted as an attempt to punish Barry for behavior that John regarded as insulting.

If you find yourself suffering under the rule of a heavy-handed executor, keep in mind that most jurisdictions in North America provide you with a legal solution. As a matter of law, the executor and the estate solicitor must act in the best interests of all the beneficiaries. So if you appeal to the estate's solicitor, and he or she is unable or unwilling to force the executor to respect your interests, you can hire another lawyer to defend them. If the executor is falsely asserting a debt, your lawyer can contest his claim in a legal proceeding. If you believe that the executor has misinterpreted a provision of the will, your lawyer can seek a judicial ruling on its meaning. If the executor fails to provide you with a copy of the will or a comprehensive list of assets, your lawyer can ask the court to order him to do so or to perform any other undischarged duty. If you have evidence to establish that your executor is hopelessly biased in his administration of the estate, your lawyer can also ask the court to replace him with an independent, unbiased party. I stress that these rights are available to you in *most* jurisdictions. To determine exactly how to protect yourself in any particular state or province, you should seek the advice of a competent estate lawyer.

I turn now to the second inheritance situation that often leads to sibling conflict.

## 2. Unequal Shares

When parents leave unequal bequests to their children, conflicts often emerge. As in the previous case, the cause of conflict is sibling rivalry resulting from the perception of parental favoritism. Since the less favored heir obviously cannot direct his anger at his parent, he directs it against his siblings. This can lead to family breakups, lawsuits and, in extreme cases, violence. (As we saw in Chapter 4 under the "I'm-Not-Worthy" Syndrome, the less-favored can also direct his anger against his bequest.)

One principal cause of unequal giving is the weakness and neediness of an elderly parent. If infirmities render an aging parent unable to survive without the assistance of others, he might make promises concerning an inheritance to secure or reward the support of one or more of his children. Sometimes conflicting promises are made, often by accident, as powers of memory and judgment diminish. A sibling can receive an awful shock, for example, when he finds that his father's promise to leave him a certain sum, out of gratitude for nursing him at home, does not materialize in the will. That sibling might be inclined to make a claim against his father's estate for his rightful compensation. Another brief example is provided in an article written by Andrea Gross for the *Ladies' Home Journal*:

> *A Los Angeles woman...told her son she had put money into trust accounts to pay for his children's college education. Later, sick and needing care that only her daughter could provide, she agreed to transfer the money to her daughter. After the woman's death, her son discovered the duplicity and was hurt and angry. Today, several years later, the differences between brother and sister are irreconcilable.*[9]

Another common cause of unequal giving is the divided loyalties that result from a parent's second marriage. If there are children from the first and second marriages, the parent will often have great difficulty determining how to distribute his estate. Frequently, the decision is made to favor the children of the second marriage since they are often younger and less established in life than the children of the first. The first children, though, are unlikely to share their parent's sympathy for the second. Receiving less than the second family is like being rejected a second time. (In some cases, it can also mark a continuation of the financial hardship that the children of the first marriage experienced when their parents separated.) The resulting anger can drive the first children to bring a suit to challenge the validity of the will. This is what the heirs of the Johnson & Johnson fortune did.

Seward Johnson, son of the founder of the multibillion-dollar conglomerate, had been a director of the company from 1921 to 1971 and was one of its principal shareholders.[10] When he died in 1983 at the age of 87, he left an immense fortune, principally comprising 7 million shares in the company. His net worth was estimated to be close to a half-billion dollars.[11]

Mr. Johnson had married his third wife, Basia, his former maid, in 1971, when he was 76 years old and she was 34. During their marriage, one of Mr. Johnson's favorite pastimes, apparently, was drafting new wills. Since 1971, he had executed 22 wills, four of which were drafted during the last 56 days of his life. Controversy ensued when five of Johnson's six children from his first marriage discovered that neither they nor their father's charitable foundation, the Harbor Branch Oceanographic Institute, had been named as beneficiaries in his last will. Instead, almost his entire estate was left to Basia. She was given a life interest in the estate, which would give her a yearly income of $50 million, and the right to select the charities that would receive the estate after her death. She was also given the right to borrow unlimited amounts from the principal and to set aside $20 million for the "descendants of her father," all of whom lived in Poland.

Seward Jr. was the only child of the first marriage to receive a bequest. He was named a co-executor, received a home on Cape Cod and $1 million, and was entitled to a seven-figure executor's fee. Nonetheless, he encouraged the other children to join him in challenging the validity of their father's will in the courts of New York. In the suit, the children argued that the final will could not have reflected their father's real intentions because it left nothing to Harbor Branch, which had been a beneficiary in every prior will. In his penultimate will, signed only a few days before the final version, he had left the institute $70 million.

The children asserted that their father had been "bullied and terrorized by his wife" during his marriage. In the final days of his life, when he was "riddled with cancer" and too weak to resist Basia, she coerced him into signing a will that made her, in effect, the sole beneficiary. The children asked the court to nullify the final will on the ground that Mr. Johnson had been the victim of "fraud, duress, coercion and undue influence" exercised by Basia and the Johnsons' lawyer, Nina Zaget. (Zaget drafted most of the recent wills and was named a co-executor, a position that potentially entailed a fee of several million dollars.)

In her defense, Basia's lawyers argued that 1) Johnson was competent and still conducting his own affairs when he signed the will; 2) he left everything to Basia out of gratitude for her showing him how to enjoy his wealth—they had spent lavish amounts on grand estates and artwork during their marriage; 3) he had already provided for his children, setting up trusts for them in 1944, thus relieving himself of any further financial obligations; and 4) he was disinclined to give them anything else because he was embarrassed by their mismanagement of their personal and financial affairs.

The suit brought by the Johnson children cannot be explained by need or greed. In her third defense, Basia correctly asserted that the children had already received considerable wealth from their father. Their trust funds had made each one of them a multimillionaire. So why did they feel compelled to contest the will? Was it really out of a concern for the institute?

The answer is that the children couldn't stomach the fact that they were left nothing while unknown relatives from the third marriage were left $20 million:

*The children were stunned and disappointed by the news.... Together, Seward Jr. testified, they decided any will that ignored both his [father's] beloved Harbor Branch and his own descendants while it provided for "a bunch of Polish people he hardly knew" couldn't possibly reflect their father's intention.*[12]

The bequest to Basia's relatives incited an inter-familial rivalry that could be extinguished only by rewriting the will. Shortly after the trial began, Basia agreed to a $159-million settlement. After paying hefty estate taxes, Seward Jr. received $12.9 million and the other children $5.9 million each. Harbor Branch received $20 million and the children's lawyers $10 million. One suspects that this settlement turned on the fact that the Johnson children were now receiving a larger share than Basia's relatives would receive.[13]

The distribution of unequal bequests among children of one marriage or between children of two marriages is one of the most damning problems faced by heirs. Unless someone can prove that a parent wasn't competent or was under duress when he or she signed the will, nothing can be done to change its terms. Children are left to work it out among themselves. Thus, the most favored heirs must decide whether holding on to their unequal shares is worth the conflicts that the resentment of the less-favored will inflict on the family. The real solution to this problem lies in the hands of the benefactor. Your parent should divide his or her estate equally or explain satisfactorily in the will the reasons for dividing it unequally. If this is not done, the final legacy can be the breakup of the family.

Let's now turn to a third inheritance situation that often produces sibling conflict.

# 3. Dividing Possessions

By the time our parents get around to writing their wills, they have acquired a large number of personal possessions such as china, furniture, automobiles, jewelry, silver and so on. The very accumulation of these possessions may have been the impetus to writing the wills. Yet parents often resist listing and assigning each possession individually because the process is time-consuming and tedious. While they might leave specific shares of less numerous liquid and capital assets to you and your siblings, they might leave their possessions to you collectively. That seems fair, and it's certainly convenient for them. Unfortunately, it leaves you with a difficult task. With the assistance of the executor, you are left to decide how to distribute the possessions to achieve equality.

The easy solution is simply to sell everything and distribute the revenue equally. That, unfortunately, is rarely a viable option. Siblings generally want to keep some of their parents' possessions for sentimental reasons. And this creates a sticky problem. Siblings must distribute the possessions in a way that satisfies the monetary equality dictated by the will. At the same time, each will want to acquire certain possessions to which he or she has a special emotional attachment. Frequently, the distribution dictated by sentiment conflicts with the distribution dictated by monetary equality. One sibling may have to give a possession to which he is strongly attached to a brother or sister to achieve that equality. And that can produce resentment and conflict.

This problem can be resolved when one sibling agrees to take a smaller share in exchange for the right to hold on to a particular possession. It can also be resolved when a sibling who wants a larger share offers to pay the other siblings for the right to take it. But how do you deal with this problem when these solutions aren't available?

One option is to turn the decision over to the executor. And, in fact, benefactors sometimes give the executor the discretionary power to distribute possessions to avoid these type of disputes. However, this solution often backfires. The executor may be ignorant of sentimental value and may assign or dissolve the possessions to achieve strict monetary equality. This usually leaves everyone dissatisfied and makes the executor the focus of conflict. Or he consults the beneficiaries and tries to satisfy their conflicting claims. However, once he does that, he is forced to reconcile emotional and financial values. Thus, we find ourselves with the same problem faced by siblings when they are left to determine the division by themselves. So, how do we solve it?

One simple and elegant solution is provided by the *Ladies' Home Journal* article that I referred to earlier. It tells the story of three sisters from Nebraska who had to divide a parent's belongings among themselves. On a scale of one to five, they rated each possession for its monetary and emotional value. Then they added the two scores to determine a composite value for each object and chose "accordingly."[14]

This approach is fine as far as it goes. However, three additional conditions would have to apply to make it truly workable. First, each participant would have to articulate his or her criteria for establishing the emotional value of an object. (For assistance in formulating them, see Chapter 7.) Second, since someone could end up with possessions that have high monetary value and little emotional value, and vice versa, everyone would have to waive the requirement of strict monetary equality. Finally, the participants would have to determine the order in which each would choose. The best way to do that might be simply to draw straws.

# 4. Battling Ghosts

One other form of family conflict deserves special attention because it is so difficult to resolve: the conflict between a dead parent and a child. It arises when a parent tries to control the life of the child from beyond the grave by means of a will that distributes benefits under stringent conditions. This kind of will takes its bearing from what is now a prohibited provision in most North American jurisdictions: the so-called *dum casta* clause. Under it, a husband could stipulate that his bequest to his wife be revoked if she remarried.

A notorious example of this kind of clause was provided a decade ago by the will of the communications magnate, Richard Eaton. When Eaton died at the age of 81 in Bethesda, Md., he left a $50-million estate consisting of radio stations, television cable systems, real estate, stocks and other securities. He divided his estate among his wives, children and grandchildren from his first and second marriages, under some unusual conditions.

His will stated that his first wife, Marguerite, who was 76 years old at the time, would receive generous living expenses during her lifetime and the right of first choice in the division of his personal possessions. However, his 44-year-old second wife, Elsa, with whom he was still living at the time of his death, was prevented from receiving her 16-percent share of the estate until the following conditions were met: Before Elsa could receive her first 8 percent, Eaton had to be dead for 10 years, and Marguerite also had to be dead. Another five years had to pass before she could receive her remaining 8 percent. Furthermore, Elsa would be disinherited if she remarried, lived with a man, or forced any of her daughters to leave home before the age of 25. Adding insult to injury, Eaton also stipulated that Elsa would lose her fortune if she violated the following injunction: "She shall not unduly harass, nor disturb my former wife, Marguerite Georgette Eaton, nor unduly interfere with her peaceful existence...." Finally, Elsa and her daughters would lose their shares if she contested the will.

Nine days after Eaton's death, Elsa challenged these provisions and won. The court ruled that Eaton's will could not override Maryland law, which provided that a surviving spouse was entitled to one-third of the estate of a deceased spouse.[15]

Although clauses such as those in the Eaton will are no longer tolerated in North America, some that share their manipulative spirit have managed to survive.

One example is a clause that makes access to wealth dependent on a child's pursuit of a particular career or life style. This often takes the form of an incentive trust. A child is given income or a capital payment from a trust fund for attaining an important career goal such as graduating from law school. The obvious evil of an incentive clause is that it might direct someone to pursue a career or life style that doesn't match his or her needs and aspirations. On the other hand, this kind of clause can sometimes be in the interest of the beneficiary because it forces him to find his place in life before coming into wealth. That ensures the wealth will not be frittered away in pursuit of false dreams.

Ascending to the ranks of a profession or spending a certain number of years in a particular position or business

is, I believe, properly taken as a sign that a child has acquired the skills and the maturity to manage an inheritance. A surrogate for these criteria is age. In this case, it's
common to find bequests staggered over a period of years.
The smallest share might be distributed when a child is in
his twenties, to assist him in completing a college degree or
some other form of vocational training. A larger share
might be released in his early forties to enable him to purchase a home and raise a family. The largest share might
come in his fifties, when he presumably has the wisdom to
preserve the wealth for his retirement and his children.

A clause that *holds back* an inheritance if someone
pursues a particular career or lifestyle can also be harmful.
Consider the case of Ted Turner. Turner's father owned a
successful billboard business in Atlanta, but shortly before
he committed suicide, he sold it because he thought Ted
wasn't fit to run it. Yet that was Ted's burning ambition.
In effect, Turner Sr. had created an estate plan that oper-
ated like a disincentive clause. By selling the business, he
transferred his wealth on the condition that Ted would
never pursue his dream of running the company. But Ted
found a way to overturn his father's decision. A few days
after the death, he convinced his mother to allow him to
use the proceeds from the sale of the business to repur-
chase it. He then approached the purchaser and persuaded
him to sell. The purchaser was sympathetic to Ted's plight
once Ted explained that keeping the business "was his one
chance to get going in life."[16]

The hardship that Ted Turner narrowly avoided can
also arise if a parent decides to disinherit a child. This is
the situation faced by the children of Warren Buffett. In
1986, Buffett announced that he will be leaving almost his
entire estate to charity, with perhaps no more than a few

hundred thousand dollars going to his son Howard and daughter Susan. Buffett isn't disinheriting them because he disapproves of their career choices or character. (When Buffett announced his intention, Susan was an administrative assistant to an editor at *U.S. News and World Report*, and Howard was a successful farmer.) He stated that his desire is to force them to "carve out their own place in this world." In the same breath, he asserted that giving his children "a lifetime supply of food stamps just because they came out of the right womb" could be "harmful" and "an anti-social act." He wanted to leave them "enough money so that they could do anything, but not so much that they could do nothing."[17]

This sounds very noble but it bespeaks a man who isn't really interested in his children's happiness. After spending their formative years learning how to live in conditions that only several billion dollars can provide, Susan and Howard are told that they will have to carry on as though they never were Warren Buffett's offspring. One has to wonder whether that won't leave them with unresolved anger toward their father. One can already hear resentment in a comment made by Susan around the time of their father's announcement. She told *Fortune* magazine:

> *...I basically agree with him. But it's sort of strange when you know most parents want to buy things for their kids and all you need is a small sum of money—to fix up the kitchen, not to go to the beach for six months. He won't give it to us on principle. All my life my father has been teaching us. Well, I feel I've learned the lesson. At a certain point, you can stop.* [18]

In 1990, Howard also indicated some discontent when he spoke to *Fortune* concerning the terms of the mortgage held by his father on his 406-acre farm. Howard has to pay his father 22 percent of the farm's gross income if he weighs 182.5 pounds or less and 26 percent if he weighs more. One can hear a tinge of bitterness in Howard's comment:

> *I don't mind it really. He's showing he's concerned about my health. But what I do mind is that, even at 22 percent, he's getting a bigger payback than almost anybody around. Somehow he always manages to control the circumstances.*[19]

Disinheritance might indeed make you energetic and determined to find your own place in the world, as Mr. Buffett hopes. However, if you developed aspirations in relation to your family's wealth, as Ted Turner certainly did, you might be terribly embittered to see it handed over to strangers. And, unlike Mr. Turner, you probably won't find any way of reversing your parent's estate plan. If you find yourself in the shoes of Susan or Howard Buffett (I'm assuming on a much smaller scale), you should be sensitive to the possibility of developing a syndromic response. As we saw in Chapter 4, under the "I'm-Too-Worthy" Syndrome, receiving less than you expected or deserved can create anger that is ultimately directed against yourself in the form of reckless financial dealing or a disastrous career move. If you see yourself moving toward either, consider seeking the advice of a mental health professional.

For those who face clauses that force them to pursue or withdraw from a particular career or life style, one solution would be to consult an estate lawyer concerning a legal challenge. The possibility of succeeding will depend on the laws in your jurisdiction.

# Strategies for Avoiding Conflict

We began this chapter with the concept of equilibrium. It holds that conflicts develop when a family member inadequately fills a role that was played by a deceased grandparent, parent or sibling. In our study of the Zeffer family, we saw how a sibling who insists on replacing a deceased parent, but doesn't have the temperament to succeed, can cause bitter conflict. Obviously, though, this doesn't always have to be the case. The displacement of roles and needs can eventually produce positive change. Some family members may have to grow up quickly and learn to satisfy certain needs on their own. Others may discover untapped potential in learning how to play new roles. In the extreme case, a family that was riven by conflict due to the actions of the deceased has an opportunity to finally come together.[20] While a clear strategy for avoiding disequilibrium and conflict following a death may not exist, we can perhaps find some solace in recognizing that loss provides an opportunity for practical and spiritual growth.

As for avoiding conflicts arising from the symptoms of grief, several clear-cut strategies do exist. One very simple tactic is to share, as much as possible, your thoughts and feelings with your family members. Openness provides the best defense against the misunderstandings that inevitably arise when a family member dies.[21] Unfortunately, though, openness can have a hidden down side. The family that communicates best is usually the family that is already very close, and that closeness can sometimes cause conflict. It can lead family members "to displace blame, anger and other hostile feelings onto one another, to avoid communication for fear of upsetting the others, or to place irrational demands on each other."[22] So both open and closed families have to make a conscious effort to keep the lines of communication open.

Another important strategy is to recognize and accept the fact that family members can grieve in different ways. If my clients Josh and Larry had realized this, Larry might not have been so offended by Josh's need to put on a happy face to avoid his grief, and Josh might have been less hurt by Larry's emotional outburst.[23]

Edward Myers, in *When Parents Die*, provides four other helpful strategies:

1. **Remember that grief heightens emotions.** You and your siblings are under stress, and your reactions even to everyday events may be more intense than usual. What seem like insoluble pro blems may look easier to solve in a few months. Don't burn your bridges.

2. **Try to keep issues separate.** A conflict over a seemingly practical issue (such as selling the family house) may have deep emotional roots. If you can perceive where one issue ends and another starts, you'll have a better chance of dealing with them successfully.

3. **Consider the possibility of an outsider's viewpoint.** You and your siblings may have such strong feelings about the aftermath of your parent's death that you may not be able to see events clearly. A trusted aunt, uncle, other relative or family friend may be able to provide insights that all of you lack. (*As we saw in Chapter 5, well-meaning relatives and friends can also cause more problems than they solve. Choose your advisers carefully.*)

4. **Be careful of speaking your mind too impulsively.** Bereavement can provide an opportunity for speaking with rare candor—an opportunity often well-worth taking. Ultimatums, dares and threats during a time of confusion, however, may drastically compound the damage your family has already suffered.[24]

I would add two recommendations to Myers's list: If your family is so riven by conflict that the estate cannot be administered, consider using a professional mediator to assist you in achieving a truce. And don't assume that the best mediator is a highly trained lawyer. The best mediator is someone who has had professional training or experience in using mediation procedures and is familiar with the financial and emotional issues that can arise in an inheritance conflict. That person might be a psychologist, a former banker, a financial consultant or a lawyer.

Second, if you are chosen to be sole executor of your parent's estate, be sure to provide your siblings with a copy of the will, a list of assets, probate documents and any other information that will help them understand how the estate will be administered. Invite questions, answer them in writing and share copies with everyone. Also, if you are given the discretionary authority to distribute possessions, use it wisely. Consult with every sibling and seek consensus on the appropriate division. If consensus isn't easily achieved, then empower your siblings to make their own decisions by adopting the rating system recommended above. Remember that for the duration of your executorship, which, on average, can last anywhere from six months to a year, you are the *de jure* leader of the family. The way in which you behave can set the tone for everyone else.

This final recommendation takes us back to the very first. Openness is the cornerstone of all other strategies. A family survives bereavement by means of dialogue and consensus, or, at the very least, dialogue. When differences and problems are not discussed, they can fester and surface later on. Suppressed anger and jealousy can cause siblings to engage in a lifetime of conflict. These emotions can also spill over into married life and the workplace where they damage other relationships. We often avoid an honest discussion of our differences, especially after a bereavement, since honesty itself often leads to conflict. That, however, is the price that sometimes must be paid in the short run to achieve a lasting reconciliation.

# Chapter 7

# The Value of a Thing

When Mary Lessing died of liver failure at the age of 56, a year after her husband had suffered a fatal stroke, her son Terry, who was then in his early 30s, and his two younger brothers, both of whom were in their early 20s, were left a considerable inheritance. A portfolio of bonds, stocks and mutual funds worth close to $600,000 was split equally between Terry's siblings and placed in trusts from which each could draw income until his 35th birthday when each would receive the principal. Terry was left the family home, worth about $240,000, and all its contents.

Although Terry was very fond of his family home, he had to sell it. It was too far from his place of business (an hour-and-a-half commute each way) to be a suitable residence. And selling would give him the cash he badly needed to start his own consulting business. Dealing with the possessions proved to be a more complicated matter.

Most of the possessions were art objects that had been handed down from mother to daughter over three generations, with each recipient adding things of her own liking to collections of china, crystal, silver and oil paintings. Mary had left all of these possessions, which were prominently displayed throughout the family home, to Terry, who was a civil engineer with an international construction company, hoping that he would marry some day, start a family and hand them down to his own children. Unfortunately, Mary's wishes didn't match her son's life style.

Terry lived in a one-bedroom apartment that was too small to accommodate the objects, he had no immediate plans to marry and buy a home where he could enjoy them and, in any event, he really had no time to use them since he was frequently overseas on business. These considerations pointed toward liquidation. On the other hand, he knew that these possessions had been handed down through the generations and, unlike his two brothers, he had always admired them. Sentiment pointed toward keeping them. What to do?

Terry's first step was to find out what the objects were really worth. He called on a family friend, Roger Bellamy, an executive salesman at an exclusive jewelry store, to perform the appraisals. Roger spent an afternoon at the family home providing detailed histories of the objects and assigning values. He spent the better part of his time examining the silver collection, which consisted of British sterling silver flatware (eight place settings), sterling candlesticks, several 18th-century plated serving dishes with ornate chasings, and a magnificent 19th-century sterling tea service. These items had been on display in a breakfront in the dining room and were used on a regular basis.

While Roger was impressed with the quality of the silver collection and gave it a total value of $20,000 to $25,000, he suggested that its various patterns were "overly busy." In fact, he reserved special disdain for the tea service, which he said was "important" but "gaudy." Roger's comments were brief but they made Terry feel that the silver collection was inelegant and not really worth keeping. That led him to offer it for sale through a well-known New York auction house.

Three months later, Terry was delighted when he received a letter from the auctioneer informing him that all the items had been seen sold; a check in the amount of $17,500 was enclosed. Later that same week, he had dinner with a neighbor who offered some timely advice about his inheritance. Without knowing that he had already sold the silver collection, she stressed the importance of holding on to his mother's things. She said, "You can always make money, but you can never replace your precious family possessions." Terry was dumbstruck by the comment. He was too embarrassed to admit what he had done.

The next morning he woke up an hour early with an awful feeling in the pit of his stomach. He was overwhelmed by guilt and regret. What had he been thinking when he decided to sell those "precious family possessions"? The sterling tea set had been his mother's most cherished possession; wouldn't she have felt disappointed and betrayed by his decision to sell it? All the silver items had been so much a part of daily life in the household; weren't they essential links to the past? How could he have treated them as mere commodities? Didn't these objects deserve to be treated as intrinsically valuable? Couldn't he have enjoyed them as art objects, signs of taste and symbols of accomplishment?

After dwelling constantly on these questions for more than a month, Terry resolved to attempt to trace the objects and buy them back. Luckily, the auctioneer was sympathetic to Terry's feelings and persuaded the purchaser of the tea set, a London dealer, to sell the set back to Terry at a modest premium. Unfortunately, the auctioneer could not trace the other items because they had been sold to private collectors who expected their transactions to remain private. Terry was grateful that the tea set had been retrieved but, for years, he harbored guilt and regret about the sale of the other objects.

Due to the size and nature of the Lessing estate, some of us may have trouble empathizing with Terry's heartbreak over selling a few items, especially given his handsome cash return. However, if that is the case, we're missing the point. Whether you inherit a silver collection, an old rocking chair or a rhinestone necklace, if the object had some sort of emotional significance, you, like Terry, will probably feel confused about what to do with it. Terry's example is important because it serves as a warning to anyone who inherits personal possessions. In most cases, you will face a choice between selling the possessions and, often with some inconvenience, keeping them. Because we aren't accustomed to thinking of family possessions as important touchstones or mementos until after a family member has died, we need to rethink how we feel about them before deciding what to do. And that takes time.

When you first comb through inherited possessions and begin to sort out how you feel about them, you may be prematurely influenced by a well-meaning friend or expert who makes his or her own preferences your standard of judgment. This, of course, is what happened to Terry when he consulted Roger. Roger made his comments in passing;

however, they held great sway over Terry because he had not fully considered the collection's sentimental value. If he had waited and consulted some of his family and friends, like the neighbor who advised him to keep his mother's precious things, eventually he would have realized that the emotional cost of selling far outweighed the monetary gain.

Terry's story thus gives us the basic formula for considering whether to keep or sell possessions. Using the guidelines in Chapter 5 for evaluating your objects; use auction and antique experts to ascertain their market value. Next, discuss the importance of the objects with family members and friends as a way of testing your own feelings about their emotional worth. (Be sure, by the way, that these friends knew your benefactor well enough to offer a sound opinion as to what he or she may have expected you to do with the objects.) Then compare the economic value to the emotional value. One or the other will eventually take pre-eminence and determine your decision.

One problem, though: While professional appraisers share a common set of criteria for establishing an object's monetary value, no one has yet defined the criteria for establishing its emotional value. You certainly won't find any helpful guidelines in textbooks on art objects, auction catalogs or estate handbooks. That's probably because most people assume that emotional worth is something too nebulous or individual to be defined or measured. I would like to suggest, on the contrary, that we can develop some simple, essential guidelines for determining how we feel about an inherited object. In the course of evaluating my own family possessions and assisting clients and friends in evaluating theirs, I have found the following questions to be very helpful in determining emotional value.

**Does an object represent a special principle or belief of the deceased?** Let's say your late father was an avid outdoorsman and left you a landscape painting that reflected his love of nature. You, on the other hand, have always hated camping and hunting and see no value in holding on to a painting that you would never display in your downtown apartment. What should you do? You might consider keeping it for one simple reason: It embodies one of your father's passions. As time goes on and memories fade, you might be very pleased to have a tangible reminder of your father's character.

**Is an object associated with the memory of an important family event?** What should you do if your mother leaves you a china set with a dated pattern that doesn't suit your taste? If that set was used regularly at family gatherings, you might wish to keep it. As the family continues to meet and share a meal during Thanksgiving and Christmas, it might serve as a touchstone linking family members to cherished memories of times spent with parents or grandparents. If, on the other hand, the family meets less frequently due to the loss of the parent who had been responsible for keeping everyone together, the china might serve the very same function. It could be a comforting reminder of better times.

**Do you feel that an object reflects your benefactor's continuing love and support?** This may seem like a rhetorical question. Isn't it obvious that an inheritance, whether it's in the form of stocks, real estate, a business or possessions, reflects your benefactor's concern for your future well-being? You might be surprised to find that you regard possessions, particularly when they don't suit your life style, as a nuisance rather than a blessing. Keep in mind, though, that you might feel quite differently once a possession has been sold. You can feel tremendous guilt because you defeated the intention of your benefactor to promote your welfare by means of a specific gift. Regret often sets in even if the object represented a misguided or shortsighted attempt to promote your welfare. You didn't really need those green and pink coffee mugs, but your grandmother thought you did; for that reason alone, you may feel better in the long run by keeping them.

One of my colleagues once had a client who understood this aspect of inheritance very well. Derrick, a soybean farmer in Ontario, had inherited a Rolls-Royce from an uncle who had been a very successful doctor in a nearby city. The Rolls certainly didn't mesh well with Derrick's way of life but he held on to it. He felt that his uncle had wanted him to share in the pleasure of his financial success by giving him what was perhaps his favorite possession. Even after Derrick had damaged the chassis in a highway accident and could not afford to repair it, he held on to the vehicle, storing it in a corner of his barn, where it still sits today. When my colleague asked Derrick why he was keeping a vehicle he couldn't afford to use, Derrick replied, "My uncle wanted me to have it, so I'm keeping it."

**Does the possession embody the importance of maintaining continuity between generations?** In aristocratic times, handing down a landed estate from father to son under the rule of primogeniture was the means of transmitting family history and traditions from one generation to the next. The possessions of the estate played an important role in forming the character of the next generation, shaping its tastes and aspirations. If, for example, the family had been distinguished for its cultivation of musical tastes, the home would probably be filled with hand-crafted instruments, lavish folios of music, paintings and sculptures depicting musicians and lovers of music, and furnishings designed to seat audiences for special perform- ances. In such an environment, the love of music easily passed from father to son.

Needless to say, it's very rare indeed to find anyone, even among the wealthiest North American families, who aspires to pass on possessions with a view to shaping the character of the next generation. Perhaps an equivalent act today is passing on the family business. However, a fam- ily business is rarely transferred successfully,[1] and even when it is, it often changes its form and substance as the next generation is forced to chart new investment strate- gies to deal with changing markets, tastes and technolo- gies, as well as new competitors. Handing on a family busi- ness certainly ensures that the next generation will be businesspeople, but it cannot guarantee what kind of busi- nesspeople they will become.

In a world where the link between property and char- acter has been broken, most of us don't think of inherited possessions as a means of maintaining continuity between generations. Nonetheless, they can still perform that func- tion to a certain degree. Precisely because we live in a world that is becoming increasingly fragmented, some people may need to hold on to inherited possessions to establish some link with the past. If family members live in different parts of the country or the world, and the opportunities for meeting are diminishing, consider keeping inherited pos- sessions as reminders of the familial beliefs and experi- ences that played a role in shaping your outlook on life.

**Do you feel that an object is the embodiment of the deceased?** Once the reality of a loss has set in, you might feel that your inherited possessions are all you have left to prove that your loved one was here. In this frame of mind, the love you can no longer share with your family member is sometimes transferred to his or her possessions. You might find yourself doting over a lounge chair, a fountain pen or a vase that previously you never cared for.

Unfortunately, many heirs decide to sell possessions before they discover the extent to which they are affected by this experience. This can lead to emotional hardship. If you feel the need to reunite with your loved one by surrounding yourself with inherited possessions, but you've already sold them, you can feel like you've lost your family member a second time. You may enter a new cycle of grieving and re-express symptoms, such as anxiety, sadness, depression and so on. In particular, you may feel extreme guilt because you were directly responsible for the loss.

Transference isn't an experience that will affect everyone to the same degree, and so we can't assume that everyone will feel that a conversion of objects is like a second bereavement. Nonetheless, you should consider waiting a year or more before deciding whether to sell possessions because that will give you time to determine how you really feel about them.

**Do the possessions reflect a way of life that is different than or similar to your own?** Under the first question addressed here, we considered what to do if you inherited an easy-to-use or easy-to-store household possession that reflects an important principle or belief of your loved one. Here I address what to do if you inherit a number of possessions or one or more high-maintenance possessions that you could keep only if you changed your own life style or living arrangements. Dealing with this problem entails defining the way of life or the ultimate value expressed by the inherited possessions and how you feel about it.

If appreciating artistry was the ultimate value for your benefactor, you might inherit heavily insured artwork or musical instruments. If a cohesive family life was the overriding value, you might receive a house full of comfortable, durable, unfashionable furnishings. If financial success was the goal, you might be left a load of glitzy, ostentatious possessions. Certainly, if you share any of the values expressed by these possessions, you would want to keep them. On the other hand, what if you're not an art aficionado, don't have a family or prefer simple appointments? You might feel your benefactor is meddling in your life by using the bequest to force you to adopt an undesired value. Your first inclination will be to convert the possessions to cash. However, that can turn out to be a mistake. There are four important reasons to hold on to objects that conflict with your way of life.

First, you might find that these possessions provide you with an opportunity to reflect on the relative merits of your own way of life and your benefactor's, particularly if your bequest came from a parent or grandparent. Perhaps you'll see these possessions as means of broadening or deepening your outlook, or simply changing it, recognizing that it has become tiresome or outmoded. Maybe, after 20 years of modest living, it's time you stopped making utility the goal of life and used your mother's art collection to learn how to appreciate beauty as an end in itself. If you were a high-liver during the 1980s, maybe those simple, solid furnishings from the family home could help you ease into a less ambitious and more comfortable life style that matches the diminishing returns of the 1990s. If you've been a successful saver and are reaching a stage in life where you and your spouse might enjoy luxury items, maybe some of those glitzy items you inherited from your grandparents could serve as a reward for all your years of hard work.

So the first reason to keep "unwanted" possessions is that you can use them as a foil to highlight how you feel about your own way of life and its material expression. You might decide that these possessions can and should be used to transform your life style.

The second reason to keep them is that they invoke one of the considerations mentioned under questions 1 through 5 listed above.

The third reason is that they can sometimes be altered or transformed to accommodate your life style. Let me present two simple examples: One of my clients, Sally Werner, inherited some high-quality furniture from her great-aunt to whom she had been very close. Most of the pieces were acquired during the 1930s and 1940s and included a mahogany dining-room set with a display cabinet and a serving table, two bedroom sets and two coffee tables, one with marble inlay. While none of the pieces had real antique value, Sally was aware that she couldn't afford to acquire contemporary pieces of similar quality. All the pieces were useful and valuable. Yet Sally found them unattractive: they had dark finishes, were slightly cumbersome and, overall, just looked old-fashioned. They would have stuck out like sore thumbs in her modern townhouse.

She was planning to consign them to an auction house when she showed them to a friend, Simone, an architect, who pointed out that if the furniture were stripped down and refinished in an imaginative way, it would be suitable for a modern setting. She had seen this done with similar pieces in a colleague's home and offered to put Sally in touch with the tradesman responsible. Sally made the contact, saw examples that excited her and decided to have all the pieces refinished, except for one bedroom set, which she sent to auction. That simple move allowed Sally to honor her aunt's bequest without compromising her own tastes.

Our second example takes us into avant-garde quarters in New York City in the late 1970s. Morris, a stage designer residing in the SoHo district, was 22 years old when his grandmother died at her home in New Rochelle. She had been a British immigrant to the United States some 30 years before but had always found it difficult to fully conform to American customs. Among her many English eccentricities was her ritual of afternoon tea, always served using her finest Wedgwood tea set. In her will, she left this prized possession to Morris, her only grandson, to remind him not to forget his British heritage. Morris was in a quandary over the gift. What was he, an intrepid member of the city's punk scene, to do with a floral-patterned five-piece tea set with 25 cups and saucers? Clearly, the set represented an essential aspect of his grandmother's character and her desire to transmit her heritage to a succeeding generation. He was inclined to keep it for these reasons, even though he couldn't see himself using it within the next 30 to 40 years. On the other hand, if sold to an antique dealer on the East Side, it would bring him much-needed rent money. Reluctantly, he was moving toward selling.

That's when his roommate, Veronique, a theater student at N.Y.U., suggested that it might be a great deal of fun, in a kitschy way, to throw some Sunday afternoon tea parties. Morris sent out invitations for an afternoon of high tea featuring the music of the Sex Pistols. The event proved quite popular with the neighborhood connoisseurs of British punk. Morris's tea bashes became a monthly ritual with leather-jacketed, earringed friends dropping by to play their latest import recordings. Morris found an unlikely way to blend his grandmother's life style with his own, one that honored his grandmother's wish to preserve the British influence in the family. Unfortunately, the spontaneous slam dance that one day wiped out half the set probably wouldn't have been much approved by Grandma.

The final reason to keep possessions that don't suit your tastes or life style is to give yourself time to consider whether they might suit your way of life in the future. For example, you may not have any need for your mother's silver flatware in your 20s, but it might be well-suited to entertaining friends when you're in your 40s. There's no harm in holding on until you're absolutely sure that you'll never use it. If you don't end up using it later, it can still be sold and will probably be worth more than when you received it. On the other hand, if you sell it and decide later that you need flatware, the cost of reacquiring a similar set or a new set would probably be much higher than the price for which you sold the original set. From the standpoint of cost alone, you're usually better off holding on to valuable possessions for a few years until you're certain that you will never use them, assuming, that is, they're not unduly expensive to maintain or store.

What many heirs don't realize is that almost any item can be safely stored for an extended period if you take the time to find the right mover and the right storage facility. Storing inherited possessions is your best defense against making a hasty sale that you'll later regret. Let me give you a few tips on the proper way to do it.

If you haven't had much experience with movers, your first assumption might be that safe transport will be provided by a large, nationally known company. That assumption often turns out to be false. While you might expect nationally known carriers to impose uniform standards on franchisees, the quality of your move ultimately depends on whether the manager of your local franchise hires personnel who know how to pack and handle a wide variety of objects with a high degree of precision and care. That means you will have to conduct an investigation to determine the quality of any mover, whether it's nationally franchised or locally owned.

You can do that by speaking to friends who may have recently moved or whose line of work brings them into contact with movers on a regular basis (real estate agents come to mind). You should also interview representatives of various companies at your home and ask them how they might pack or handle unusual objects such as a grand piano or a grandfather clock and fragile objects such as china or crystal. You'll get a range of answers that will tell you pretty quickly who the most careful movers are. Also, during the interview, be sure to ask whether the company specializes in moving certain objects, such as a piano, and how much experience it has had moving other objects that might require special handling. You might want to divide moving responsibilities between companies, assigning special objects to carriers that have the requisite expertise.

Another way to find out which companies can handle special objects properly is to inquire about moving procedures with repair shops or specialty stores. Let's use the example of the grandfather clock. Before deciding which mover to use, you should contact the local jeweler who has repaired the clock in the past or any other jeweler who has had experience with similar clocks and ask him to examine it to determine whether he should remove or secure certain parts, such as the weights or pendulum, prior to the move. He might provide the essential information and services needed to ensure that the moving company does the job the right way. Also, ask him to recommend a mover with whom he has worked successfully in the recent past. In the case of a piano, contact the dealer from whom it was originally purchased, or a dealer who offers the same make, and find out who he uses to move his own merchandise. That's often the quickest route to narrowing the field of potential companies. Once you've chosen a company believing it will provide the safest move, you might also assume that it has the safest storage facility. This is often true, but sometimes it isn't. You should visit the facility and examine how and where your possessions will be stored before making any decision.

To determine the quality of the facility, you should be able to answer all the following questions. (The correct answers are in parenthesis.) Does the facility have special storage compartments that will keep your objects separated from everyone else's? (Yes. I know of one art storage company that is facing multiple law suits because it stored the paintings of several clients in the same compartment and then mistakenly sent some works to the wrong owner, who now cannot be located.) Does the facility use high-quality packing materials? (Yes. Your most valuable possessions should be wrapped in plastic bubble wrap and packed in boxes filled with Styrofoam peanuts.) Will the facility ever move your objects to make room for the possessions of new clients or to retrieve the possessions of existing clients? (No.) If possessions have to be moved in-house for any reason, does the facility have the proper equipment to make the move safely? (Yes. If your things are stored in high places, be sure that the facility has an elevating platform that can safely accommodate one or two movers and your possessions.) Does the facility monitor and maintain temperature and humidity values to ensure that every possession is preserved in its original form? (Yes. Keep in mind that dry conditions can be deadly to a piano or antique furniture.) Does the facility have a high-quality alarm system and appropriate fire prevention systems? (Yes. If you are unsure about the quality of the systems, contact your insurance agent and ask whether they are well-regarded within the insurance industry.) Are containers and individually stored objects audited on a regular basis to ensure that nothing has disappeared? (Yes. If the facility doesn't provide this service, every six months you should perform the audit yourself.)

Just as you should employ different movers depending on their expertise in handling particular objects, you should choose storage facilities on the same basis. If you wish to store art objects, you should seek out a facility that specializes in them. A good facility should give you an enclosed space from which your objects will never be moved. It should, of course, also meet all the other criteria listed previously. For furniture and other objects that don't fall into the art/antique category, you won't need a dedicated facility. You should, nonetheless, apply the same criteria. An unheated facility, for example, is unsuitable for any kind of long-range storage, so keep climate control high on your list of requirements.

One requirement you may have to drop for general storage is the prohibition on moving your containers. Since they will probably be stacked in such a facility, they will have to be moved from time to time to allow customers to retrieve possessions in containers placed below or behind yours. To minimize the number of moves, you should have your containers placed among other containers that are also slated for long-term storage. As well, you should go to the warehouse to observe the loading of your possessions into the containers. This is really the only way to ensure that they are properly secured against movement and breakage during in-house transport, which, by the way, is generally done by forklift.

One final matter to consider is insurance. You'll find that most warehouses will offer to insure your possessions through their own carriers. If you do some comparison shopping, you'll also find that warehouse rates are almost always higher than rates offered by your own insurance company or an independent broker. In fact, the cheapest way to insure your items is to have them covered as household possessions under your homeowner's or tenant's policy.

You should consider storing any possession that might have any of the emotional values we considered under questions 1 to 6 because, in spite of what you may have heard, cost is not normally an obstacle. Unless you've inherited extremely valuable art objects, your storage costs should be fairly reasonable. For example, if you're a renter, the rates should be much less than the cost of leasing the extra space you would need to use and display the possessions in your dwelling. In most cases, the cost of storage will be minimal compared to the emotional cost of selling off possessions that resonate with personal or familial meaning. Storage gives you the time to discover whether those meanings exist and thus the time you need to make a thoughtful decision about whether to incorporate inherited possessions in your way of life or dissolve them.

Always remember: Failing to hold on to possessions that have sentimental value can lead to a lifetime of recrimination and regret. The basic rule for all heirs is to hold on to any possession you think you may want. It can always be sold, but once sold, it's gone forever.

# Chapter 8

# The Meaning of Loss

The thesis of *How to Inherit Money* is that the experience of inheritance produces contradictory attitudes that can cause someone to mismanage an inheritance. In the previous seven chapters, my main goal has been to illustrate how the symptoms of grief and affluence can undermine the attitudes needed to effectively discharge your financial responsibilities. In Chapters 3 and 4, we saw that symptoms such as anxiety, anger, guilt, vanity, gratitude, loneliness, jealousy, fear and self-confusion can manifest as syndromes that cause financial loss. As you read these chapters, you might have detected one of these syndromes early enough to avoid financial loss. On the other hand, you might have found yourself in the shoes of one of my clients and discovered your syndrome after it had already caused financial hardship. If that's the case, you might ask: What good does it do to read about my mistake after the fact? In this chapter, I will provide you with three answers to that question.

On the most basic level, examining a syndrome in the wake of a disaster, even if that proves to be painful, can help you understand that your loss might not have been simply the result of irresponsibility, selfishness, greed or stupidity. To the outside world, these vices might very well have appeared to be the cause of your financial error. That might have been the criticism offered by family members if they were affected by your mistake. Certain friends and acquaintances might have said the same thing; that was their reward for the envy they experienced when they first learned about your windfall. Giving in to the diagnosis of the outside world can leave you with guilt, self-reproach and a lack of confidence in your abilities.

You can relieve yourself of these feelings only by examining your inner world. By pinpointing your symptoms and recognizing how they clouded your judgment, you can understand that your behavior was more complex and subtle than it first seemed. You may have been irresponsible, reckless, selfish or greedy, but you might discover that those qualities are foreign to your character. Lurking beneath an apparent defect might be unresolved anger or guilt about an ambivalent relationship with the deceased, guilt about receiving more than you expected, a wild self-defeating anxiety about loss, or the self-confusion that grief always produces. Understanding the deeper causes of your financial loss doesn't relieve your responsibility for it, but it can help you to see that you aren't the foolish person everyone thinks you are. You might have been weakened by your symptoms, but they will pass and so will the irrational qualities they can elicit. Realizing this can absolve your guilt, renew your self-respect and restore faith in your abilities.

The second basic benefit of becoming aware of a harmful attitude is that you can prevent yourself from slipping back into the bad habits that caused your first loss. Assuming that your loss wasn't total, this awareness can be the key to making up for your past loss by practicing sound financial management in the present.

If these are the two benefits you've taken from the book so far, then you have gained a degree of self-insight that will assist you in overcoming syndromes and managing your inheritance more prudently. These are significant accomplishments; yet they also seem limited. The lessons learned from self-examination turn out to be useful only during the time it takes to resolve a syndrome. Thereafter, they are irrelevant to the conduct of one's life. While this has been true for some of my clients, others have found that the process of self-examination produced greater insights that permanently changed their lives for the better. This is the third benefit of examining a syndrome. In asking the question, "Why did I behave this way?", a client has sometimes been forced to reflect on how his or her character was shaped by the deceased or by some other important relationship or experience. As we saw under the Syndrome of Dependency in Chapter 3, this is what happened to Leo Feldman.

Leo lost the greater part of his inheritance because he delegated the entire management of his bequest to an unethical agent and other irresponsible professionals. Reflecting on the chain of events leading to his loss, Leo recognized his mistake and from there was led to a more comprehensive reflection on the development of his own character. He realized that his mishandling of his inheritance had been caused by his ambivalent relationship with his late father. Leo had always been resentful toward his father, whose demanding career had made him an absentee parent and whose rigid attitudes had made him critical of Leo's desire to pursue a career in music. Over the years, Leo and his father had inflicted innumerable unkind words and deeds on each other. Because Dr. Feldman died suddenly, Leo had been left with unresolved guilt about their relationship. Ignoring his inheritance had resulted from a need to avoid dealing with anything that would remind him of his guilt. Leo's insight about this aspect of his grief had led to an important insight about his character, which, in turn, led to a critical moment of self-transformation.

Armed with self-knowledge, Leo had to ask himself, "How can I live better with this insight?" The immediate and, one might say, limited response was to take personal control of his financial affairs to prevent further losses. The greater response was to change fundamentally his attitude toward money and success. His staggering loss taught him to respect the time and effort his father had devoted to financial matters; he resolved to imitate his father's prudent financial practices. That change in character became the personal meaning of Leo's bereavement and his financial loss, as well as his posthumous reconciliation with his father. We saw similar responses in two other cases studies. Under the "I'm-Not-Worthy" Syndrome in Chapter 3, Vern Halliday's reflections led him from selfish hedonism to charitable giving; under the "I'm-Too-Worthy" Syndrome, Lon Ellis's reflections moved him from a miserable career and criminal wrongdoing to a therapeutic search for a way to reform his life. These cases prove that the key to overcoming the pain and guilt that follow from mismanaging or wasting an inheritance is to discover the personal meaning of the loss. That allows you to find the saving grace in your misadventures.

These cases also provide a missing clue to solving the mystery of how we can overcome the most common symptom of grief: self-confusion. I say the missing clue because the critical literature we examined in Chapter 2, which presents the resolution of grief in four stages, doesn't tell us how, exactly, we're supposed to resolve self-confusion. In Stage One, we learn to accept the reality of loss; in Stage Two, to examine all the attributes of our symptoms; in Stage Three, to survive without the support and skills of the deceased; in Stage Four, to put our energies into new activities and relationships. Stages Three and Four really concern themselves with learning to play new roles, and in that sense, describe the result of resolving self-confusion. Yet none of the stages tells us how we are to achieve that resolution. We aren't told how to make the transition from experiencing and examining our symptoms of grief to overcoming self-confusion to pursue new forms of self-definition.

Here, our three case studies re-enter the picture—they explain how this transition can be made. Again, as we saw in the case of Leo Feldman, using the symptoms of his grief as keys to unlocking the secrets of his character, Leo was inevitably led to wonder how he could lead a better life. The answer consisted in changing an attitude and learning to play the role of a prudent businessman. Although Leo's financial problems were not caused by self-confusion, but rather by unresolved anger toward his father, his resolution of that anger can serve as a model for anyone who experiences self-confusion. His experience shows us that we can define ourselves by asking the question, "How can I live better with this insight?" In other words, the Feldman case, as well as the Taylor and Ellis cases, suggests that the best way to resolve self-confusion is to reflect on the personal meaning of a loss.

This kind of reflection turns out to be the essential pre-condition to resolving the most common symptom of grief and thus one of the keys to restoring the habits and attitudes that contribute to the sound management of an inheritance. With a renewed sense of self, you can cope successfully with the new freedom that sudden wealth can bring. In gaining wisdom about your most important goals, you can develop an investment strategy that is dedicated to your real needs and aspirations, thereby overcoming the danger of wasting your inheritance on false ambitions.

It would appear that we now have a complete answer to the problem posed by the thesis of the book. We can resolve the contradiction in the experience of inheritance—the opposition between symptoms of grief and affluence and attitudes contributing to sound financial management—by discovering the personal meaning of loss. And, as I said before, if that discovery is made only after you've wasted some or all of your inheritance, it still remains the essential moment in overcoming your personal and financial losses. It can salve your pain by showing you that your losses revealed the secret of how to lead a better life.

At this point, though, you might feel that our answer to the problem of inheritance is still incomplete. You might ask: Isn't self-confusion resolved, or to put it another way, isn't self-understanding achieved only by understanding the meaning of loss in the greater scheme of things?

Answering the questions "Why did I behave this way?" and "How can I live better with this insight?" certainly gives most people the information they need to make sound decisions concerning the management of an inheritance. Yet some people might feel that the meaning culled from the examination of a personal history isn't sufficient to satisfy the longing for understanding. The urgency of this feeling is often dictated by the magnitude of our suffering. The greater the suffering, the greater the need for understanding.

If, for example, a family member suffered terribly before dying, you might ask why he or she deserved this fate. You might also ask this about yourself: Why did I have to suffer greatly by watching my loved one suffer? Whether you consider the point of suffering from the perspective of your loved one or yourself, you might very well feel the need to ask, in the words of Rabbi Harold Kushner, why bad things happen to good people. This question becomes most pressing when financial disaster follows a bereavement, as it often does. Experiencing financial loss seems unjust and inexplicable when it follows on the heels of a painful bereavement.

We cannot explain why bad things happen to good people only by reflecting on the way in which we grieved for our loss. That problem invites us to consider whether our suffering has a higher meaning or is directed by a higher force. So I turn now to Shakespeare's most famous play, *Hamlet*. It is well-suited to our purpose because, if treated as a case study, it reveals ideas that speak directly to the problem of resolving extreme grief.

Hamlet was 30 years old when his father, the king of Denmark, died suddenly. At the time, Hamlet, who was studying abroad in the town of Wittenberg, was told that the king had died accidentally; apparently, he had been bitten by a poisonous snake while napping in the palace courtyard. Although Hamlet was the king's only son and next in line to be considered for the throne, he returns home to find that his uncle, Claudius, has managed to install himself as the new king. Claudius has also married his mother, the reigning queen.

Hamlet takes up residence at the palace while suffering multiple losses: the death of his father, the loss of his kingdom and, in some sense, the loss of his mother, who, in shamelessly marrying her brother-in-law after the king's death, has become a different person in Hamlet's eyes. Losing almost everything that matters to him in the space of two months, Hamlet wanders aimlessly about the palace in the throes of extreme grief. His condition is then worsened by further horrifying news.

The king appears as a ghost to inform Hamlet that his death was not accidental; Claudius poisoned him in pursuit of a plan to steal the throne. This discovery leads Hamlet to embark on a dual mission: He must avenge his father's death by killing Claudius and claim the kingdom as rightful heir.

Burdened by the ghost's news and the demands of revenge, Hamlet's anguish becomes so great that he appears to others as though he has lost his mind. In fact, what others mistake as insanity is Hamlet's expression of extreme grief. Hamlet exhibits, in his very first speech, two major symptoms that have dogged so many inheritors. Reflecting on the loss of his father, as well as his mother's marriage to the new king, Hamlet feels that life has become unbearable:

> *O, that this too too sullied flesh would melt,*
> *Thaw, and resolve itself into a dew!*
> *Or that the Everlasting had not fix't*
> *His canon 'gainst self-slaughter. O God! O God!*
> *How weary, stale, flat, and unprofitable*
> *Seem to me all the uses of this world!*[1]

Hamlet's grief expresses itself in a melancholy so intense that the whole world seems worthless and uninspiring. Hamlet is so depressed that he can't see a present or a future worth living. This, as we know from Chapter 2, is one of the primary symptoms of extreme grief. The second symptom, also covered in Chapter 2, is Hamlet's lack of self-concern. Hamlet's grief makes him long for death—for "this too too sullied flesh" to melt. At other points, Hamlet also expresses many of the basic symptoms described by modern therapists, such as sadness, yearning, anger and preoccupation with the deceased. Strikingly, in further agreement with modern therapists, Shakespeare presents self-confusion as the fundamental symptom of Hamlet's grief. His self-confusion is revealed as a chronic inability to resolve the issue of the personal meaning of his losses. Hamlet cannot decide whether to respond to his losses by abandoning a life of contemplation for a life of political action; whether to remain a scholar or become a ruler.

Hamlet's self-confusion deserves our attention because of the way in which he tries to resolve it. His profound grief forces him to move from considering the personal meaning of his losses to what we might call the ultimate or higher meaning. In fact, the resolution of the issue of personal meaning, and thus the resolution of his self-confusion, turns on the issue of higher meaning.

In six separate speeches, Hamlet samples three fundamentally different ways of understanding the meaning of his insufferable losses. Each understanding is based on a comprehensive reflection about our place in the universe and what that tells us about how we should conduct ourselves in extreme situations. Each perspective provides Hamlet with a different version of what it means to be virtuous. He tries to find guidance on how he should deal with his situation by reflecting on these different models of human excellence. Sometimes, he adopts the outlook of the ancient pagan world where heroism was seen as the peak of human achievement. In that frame of mind, he fancies himself a spirited hero, like Achilles, whose highest purpose is to wreak vengeance on his enemies. This view counsels political action: Hamlet should kill Claudius and claim the throne. At other times, he adopts the Christian perspective and takes his bearing from a concern with the fate of the soul. This view doesn't point away from political action but it dictates the terms on which such action can be taken. (For example, when Hamlet is presented with the perfect opportunity to kill Claudius—he happens upon the king when he is alone, kneeling in prayer—he refuses to strike from fear that the king's prayers will save his soul from purgatory.) Finally, he also imitates the philosopher, who feels the need to examine every perspective. This outlook leads away from action of any kind. Since reason reveals that every perspective contains problems and contradictions, Hamlet cannot find a view that would serve as a worthy guide to action.

The lesson that we must take from Hamlet is that, for those who suffer from extreme grief, the self-insight that leads to sound financial judgment is attained by taking the time to examine and answer fundamental questions about the purpose of life itself. Sometimes financial wisdom is acquired only by acquiring wisdom itself.

I don't mean to use this observation to push our inquiry onto an abstract, impractical plane. In fact, it might very well force you to consider some of your most basic, down-to-earth experiences. It might take you back to the beginning, to early childhood memories, like the ones I shared with you in Chapter 1. In my own case, growing up in a small town with the privileges and challenges that only wealth can provide proved to be the starting point for a greater reflection on the meaning of things. These experiences would lead me to love the truth, to study philosophy and, finally, to write this book.

# In Defense of Inheritance

## Elvis and the Constitution

When Elvis Presley died at the age of 42 in 1977, he left his entire estate in trust to his 11-year-old daughter, Lisa Marie. His will stipulated that she would receive the proceeds of the estate when she turned 25, though her chances of inheriting anything seemed remote. Through excess and mismanagement, Elvis had squandered the greater part of his fortune, leaving behind $5 million in rapidly dwindling assets. Graceland was a major drain on the estate, with annual maintenance costs of around $480,000. The future looked bleak until Priscilla Presley became the estate's co-trustee, replacing Elvis's father who died shortly after Elvis. Priscilla pursued an investment strategy that would turn the declining estate into a gold mine.

The cornerstone of her strategy was to make Graceland into a tourist attraction. Investing the last $500,000 of the estate's liquid assets in the home, she opened it to the public in 1982. The investment was recouped in the first 38 days of operation. (Graceland went on to attract around 675,000 visitors and an estimated $10 million annually.) A year later, Priscilla took advantage of a new state law that gave the heirs of a celebrity property rights in the celebrity's name and image. She made a bundle licensing rights to produce Elvis memorabilia. She also struck a lucrative new royalties deal with RCA to reissue anthologies of the King's recordings.

When Lisa Marie finally inherited the estate outright in 1993, it was worth an estimated $100 million and generated $15 million annually.[1] Did Lisa Marie deserve to inherit this fantastic sum or should most of it have been taxed away by state and federal governments? To answer this question, we need to refer to the U.S. Constitution.

The Constitution guarantees every citizen the right to life, liberty and the pursuit of happiness, and in the framers' minds, the pursuit of happiness meant the acquisition and use of property. Perfecting this intention required two amendments. The Fifth Amendment guarantees that an individual's property cannot be taken by the state for a public purpose without just compensation. This provision applies when, for example, the government needs to acquire a tract of farmland to build a new highway. The government must pay a fair price for the land before gaining title to it. We can explain the duty to pay a fair price only if we assume that the state cannot claim any prior interest in the land. The government must pay full value for the asset because the individual has the complete, undivided ownership of it.

The Fourteenth Amendment, which states that a citizen cannot be deprived of life, liberty or property without due process of law, also secures the individual's right of ownership. This amendment rests on the assumption that the individual has an exclusive claim to his assets; that is the only way to explain why the states must find a strong legal justification, such as criminal wrongdoing, before depriving anyone of his or her property.

The idea that animates these two amendments is that government exists only to secure and protect each person's inherent right to acquire, use and dispose of money, goods and other possessions. That inherent right can be called a natural or inalienable right because it belongs to everyone by virtue of his membership in the human race. Any being who shares our nature must also enjoy this right. So understood, we must believe that the right existed before government was ever formed and that one of the main reasons to form and support a government is to protect this fundamental right. As James Madison put it in *The Federalist Papers*, the "first object of government" is "the protection of different and unequal faculties of acquiring property."[2]

To develop a convincing defense of inheritance, we must first prove that we do have a natural right to private property, for without it, we cannot establish an absolute right to dispose of our property while living or to transfer it at death. One might expect to find a defense of private property where the Constitution is studied—in the nation's law schools. However, today, that is where one can least expect to find someone to defend it. Most of North America's legal scholars take their bearing from philosophies that deny the existence of natural rights. The prevailing view is that the state has the ultimate right to control the distribution of property; this means that the right to inherit can be abolished at the whim of the government.[3]

## The Philosophy of Natural Right

To find the case for believing in a citizen's absolute right to acquire and transfer property, we have to return to the liberal philosophy that influenced the framers of the Constitution. The liberal philosopher whose writings perhaps had the most profound impact on the framers was John Locke. Locke's teaching in his *Second Treatise on Government* that "no one ought to harm another in his Life, Health, Liberty or Possessions" was the inspiration for the guarantee of life, liberty and the pursuit of happiness, the guarantee of the right to private property, and many other basic constitutional maxims.[4]

Locke begins his teaching with a principle that speaks to our universal interest in living safely and living well. He argues that those common interests would lead each one of us to recognize that everyone has a natural right to *comfortable self-preservation*. However, we cannot enjoy this right unless we have the *means* to enjoy it. We must have some way of acquiring the things that ensure our well-being or the right to it is useless. So Locke argues that the right to comfortable self-preservation necessarily gives us a right to acquire and transform the products of nature, and labor is what gives us title.

At first, this idea poses a problem because Locke takes the side of modern-day environmentalists and argues that nature is owned in common. Thus, to take anything from nature, we need everyone's consent or we must share whatever we take with everyone else. Locke argues that we must reject both these options because each would prevent anyone from using nature to preserve himself. By the time you asked everyone else for permission to eat the apple you just picked, it would have rotted. If you bypassed consent and sought instead to share the apple with everyone else, your share would be so small that you would starve. The only way out of this dilemma is to give each person an absolute individual right to acquire land and transform its products. But note that we are entitled only to as much land as we need to preserve ourselves and to pursue happiness. The rest belongs to all other people for their survival and happiness.

If we are entitled to as much land as we need to live in simple comfort, each of us would end up with roughly the same amount of property. The small farmers who lived on the frontiers of the early West would be Locke's model citizens. However, only for brief moments have societies ever followed the limits established by natural right. Every civilized society is and has been characterized by great inequalities in wealth, with a minority controlling most of the productive assets, including the land.

Given that inequality is a practical reality, Locke is forced to ask whether it can ever be justified. Surprisingly, his answer is yes. Extreme inequality can be justified if it enhances the right to personal security and the right to pursue happiness, the two rights that are contained within the right to comfortable self-preservation. But how is that possible? Isn't it clear that when a small group of people control the wealth of a society, they leave less for everyone else, depriving them of security and personal freedom? On the contrary, Locke argues that concentrations of wealth produce greater wealth and freedom for the entire society. We can recognize the truth of this argument, according to Locke, when we reflect on *the* fundamental problem that we face as human beings: The world is a hostile place. Nature is hostile to our aspirations. To use nature for our benefit, we must attack and subdue it. Nature gives us plenty only if we invest it with our labor.

Labor is so important to the fulfillment of our needs that nature is dwarfed in comparison. Labor increases the value of nature a hundredfold, and in many cases a thousandfold. So, the political problem for Locke becomes, how can we encourage people to mix their labor with nature to "increase the common stock of mankind"?

The solution is already in our midst. Society must introduce a currency. With money, people can acquire more land than is required for their immediate needs because they can exchange the surplus product, which is perishable, for a form of wealth that is imperishable. Money creates the possibility of accumulating personal wealth, which is *the* incentive we need to accelerate the conquest of nature or, to put it in more modern terms, to promote economic growth.

Obviously, this development leads to growth for some; that is, for those (the industrious and rational) who cornered the market on land and other capital assets. Yet everyone else is also better off, at least potentially, due to the division of labor that results. Those who do not own land find jobs working on the land itself or transforming its products. The members of this latter group, even though they are completely separated from the means of production, become guarantors of prosperity. Because others are monopolizing the society's productive resources, this group is forced to be energetic, creative and innovative in pursuit of finding ways of adding value to what the owners and their employees produce. Its ability to add value to primary products plays an essential role in promoting economic growth. The most recent development confirming the truth of Locke's teaching is the advent of computer technology. Today, the greatest value added to products is not provided by owners of land and other forms of capital, or their employees, but rather by an independent ownerless class of software specialists. They provide the expertise without which no company can compete in national or global markets.

So the monopoly held by some on the land and, later, other capital assets is justified because it creates the condition for economic development, which makes everyone better off. When inequalities exist, everyone has a better chance of securing his or her life, liberty and happiness. This is the original trickle-down theory of economic growth.

We might agree that most people are better off in societies that have adopted Locke's free-market approach, a fact that has been proved by the dynamic growth recently experienced in so many Asian countries. Yet we must also recognize that some people end up as losers in such societies. One need only spend a day walking the streets of New York City, dodging the homeless and penniless, to understand that harsh reality. Some of the champions of capitalism believe that this proves the justice of the Lockean system. Those who worked hard and trained well were rewarded and those who didn't were punished, as they should be. The critics of capitalism believe that the persistence of poverty proves the injustice of the system. Many of those who were qualified and industrious were ignored, laid off or underpaid, and then left to fend for themselves because the system doesn't always recognize the need to help the disadvantaged.

Both the champions and the critics fail to realize that Lockean liberalism is not nearly so harsh. Indeed, Locke maintains that what anyone earns or acquires by his own labor is the product of his own talent, creativity, industry; as such, no one else can claim a share in it. This means that immense inequalities of wealth that result from individual effort are insulated from state control. But let's be clear about what we mean by state control. A liberal democratic state cannot confiscate or dictate the use of any citizen's property. Yet it may "regulate" the use of property, and the forms of regulation that fall short of the impermissible extreme are numerous.

To understand how public control reenters the picture, we must return to Locke's teaching about natural rights. Remember that the right to comfortable self-preservation is the primary right in Locke's system. The right to the fruits of one's labor is a secondary right that secures the first. So, if the exercise of the right to acquire and use property does not guarantee to everyone the bounty needed to secure comfortable self-preservation, the state has a right, and in fact a duty, to tax the rents and income accruing from capital and labor to provide for the disadvantaged. (Note, however, that the state remains the judge of how much redistribution is needed to achieve the comfortable self-preservation of every citizen.)[5]

## Natural Right and Inheritance

Now that we've established the limits of the right to private property in the liberal philosophy that informs the Constitution, we can determine how they affect inheritance. Someone might say that an heir doesn't have a right to inherited wealth because he didn't earn it; labor is the only title to property in Locke's system. Yet that position, which is very popular among certain academic thinkers, looks at the issue from only one perspective, that of the recipient. We also need to see it from the standpoint of the donor. Since the original owner enjoys a right to employ his wealth as he sees fit, which we must allow on Locke's principles, he must have the right to give it away. The right to use necessarily includes the right to bequeath.[6] And so, the question is not whether a daughter deserves to receive an inheritance, but whether her father has a right to give it away. Since he does, she must have a right to receive it.

Now, even though we can find a right to inherit in liberal philosophy, we have to face another objection to the right that is based on the theory underlying a will. The act of giving presupposes a living owner who can form an intention to transfer his property and then act on it. So, when someone dies and he can no longer form an intention to use his property, he should lose his ability to give it away. And yet a will still allows him to do so. Since it takes effect only after its author has died, it extends his intention past the point where it actually exists. A will is a convenient fiction.

Critics of inheritance point to this fact to prove that every individual's property becomes ownerless after his death and therefore becomes the property of the state. This is how they justify breaching the liberal prohibition against the public confiscation of private property. While I agree that a person's property becomes ownerless after his death, a fact that no written will can change, it does not follow that the property automatically becomes a public possession. In fact, the property remains exactly as the critics first describe it—ownerless. It belongs to no one. It cannot be passed to the state or to the family of the deceased. If it didn't belong to either before his death, why would it belong to either afterward? Logically, it should be stored or destroyed. However, precisely due to its owner-less character, it becomes difficult to determine who would have the right to do either.

Some writers have sought to rescue us from this di-lemma by restoring the notion that we own all of nature and its products in common. If we originally take our pos-sessions from the common store of nature, then, when we can no longer own them, they must return to it so they can again become available to everyone else. The only practical way to ensure this outcome is to give the state the right to sell every inheritance and use the proceeds for public expenditures.

This position fails to consider Locke's argument that we must give up our common ownership of nature when we enter political society or we can never use nature to our advantage. The right of common ownership could be rein-stated only if inheritance interfered with the promise of greater overall welfare that was promised in exchange for giving up that right. And, as we shall see presently, that would be a hard argument to make.

At any rate, the problem of an ownerless inheritance is easily overcome if we reconceive a will as a gift that is transferred the moment before someone dies. And this move can be justified on Lockean grounds. If the state doesn't allow gifts prior to death or just before death, then prop-erty becomes useless and unproductive. The only way to keep it useful to others is to allow it to be spent or trans-ferred. And in the case of transfers, we shouldn't be overly concerned that a son might receive a windfall gain. Since the inherited assets can remain productive in his hands, the transfer meets the Lockean test.

# Inheritance and Equal Opportunity

At this point, many of you will have already raised an objection. Allowing parents to transfer assets to their children might indeed promote the stability and thereby the productivity of assets and businesses. However, increasing the GNP isn't the only goal worth pursuing in a liberal society. Among other things, we must be concerned with how wealth is distributed. The freedom to pursue happiness cannot be enjoyed by every citizen unless each is given an equal opportunity to pursue his dreams. That principle is rendered meaningless unless each person can attain a financial state that allows him to choose meaningfully.[7] Critics of inheritance often argue that inherited fortunes will undermine this principle because heirs will monopolize resources and the opportunities that accrue from them.

This position has been strengthened by recent research revealing that the concentration of income and wealth among the richest members of North American society reached extraordinary levels during the 1980s. From 1977 through 1987 the average after-tax income of the top 10 percent of income earners rose by 24.4 percent; the top 1 percent by 74.2 percent.[8] This in turn showed up in very high concentrations of wealth among the rich. As I noted in Chapter 1, the wealthiest 20 percent of American families now controls 80 percent of the nation's wealth. (In Canada, the top 20 percent controls approximately 70 percent of national wealth.)[9] By far the greatest gains in net worth were experienced by the top 1 percent or even half of 1 percent of the population. In 1981, there were 600,000 millionaires in the United States; by 1989, their number had risen to 1.5 million. Within roughly the same period, the number of people worth $10 million went from around

39,000 to 100,000, the number worth $100 million went from 400 to 1,200, and the number of billionaires rose from 13 to 51.

If this wealth is passed on successfully to the next generation, the critics fear the rise of a new aristocracy whose members will enjoy the lion's share of future growth. This concern becomes more pronounced when we recall that income growth has already stalled for the middle class, and we recognize that the bottom 10 percent of wage earners saw their average income fall by 10.5 percent during the 1980s.[10] Critics believe the only way to preserve equal opportunity is to allow the state to appropriate and redistribute inherited wealth. In fact, they employ the same logic to argue for a public right to control earned wealth.

Locke would argue that this criticism is based on a misunderstanding of the degree to which one can hope for equal opportunity in a liberal society. Such a society has one minimal goal: to secure everyone's comfortable self-preservation. The plenty that allows that goal to be attained can be achieved only by giving the industrious and rational few the incentive to develop the nation's resources. And the only way to guarantee that is to allow them to accumulate property and other forms of wealth. In such a world, everyone, including the bottom one-third of society, will be better off. Only the protection of private wealth fosters the growth that creates opportunities and the public revenue that provides each person with the resources and entitlements to pursue them. Locke's system provides every citizen with a better chance of realizing his potential, to pursue happiness however understood, because everyone is better off financially than he would be under any other possible arrangement.

Now the acid test for Locke's argument is whether concentrations of wealth really have been consistent with a steady and widely shared growth in employment and income. In general, the history of North American capitalism suggests that they have been. However, if it can be proved that concentrations of wealth are interfering with growth or skewing it in favor of a minority, a liberal government would be obliged to reduce their impact. It could redistribute wealth by taxing employment and investment income or by breaking up monopolies and oligopolies to make room for others to own capital and share in its growth. These two strategies, of course, have been cornerstones of the modern welfare state. And insofar as they aim at ensuring that growth is generally shared, they are legitimate forms of regulation.

Even if the critics accepted this defense, they could still raise one other concern about equal opportunity. If a capitalist aristocracy does emerge and becomes self-perpetuating by means of inheritance, no one will be able to aspire to super-wealth unless he was born into it. Locke's response to this objection is simple. He doesn't promise that everyone can begin with the same advantages or achieve the same results. He does promise, though, that the liberal state can create the economic conditions that give everyone a running chance to join in the race for success, including the race for super wealth. No other system can do as much.

Locke aside, recent studies and strong anecdotal evidence suggest that the concern about a closed aristocracy is misplaced; for many, membership in the wealthy class is relatively short-lived. Academics and business writers have argued that the wealthiest Americans receive somewhere between 45 and 67 percent of their assets from inheritance, with most agreeing that the average is around

50 percent.[11] Certainly, we can't believe mobility is a problem when 50 percent of the wealthiest earned their way to the top in one generation.

Should we, then, still be concerned that the other 50 percent inherited their wealth? Provisionally, at least, I would suggest that we shouldn't be. The question of whether this group represents a self-perpetuating class has yet to be determined. Answering the question decisively would require tracing the history of great fortunes in the United States from at least the late nineteenth century onward. We know that some fortunes have survived at least three generations—the Fords, Kennedys, Duponts and Rockefellers prove that. However, they might be the exception rather than the rule. Yale business historian Peter Dobkin Hall argues that the history of modern family businesses suggests that only 30 percent of the businesses survive to the second generation, and just 20 percent make it to the third.[12]

In fact, the dynamics of inheritance in a liberal state tend to militate against the long-term survival of great fortunes for at least four reasons. First, since wealth is constantly divided among multiple heirs in each generation, the tendency is for fortunes to peter out over time. Second, that tendency is aided and abetted by children and grandchildren of moguls who often waste their inheritances because they lack the initiative, commitment and insight of their ancestors. Third, the original source of wealth can easily be lost in a market economy from a failure to adjust and transform a business to deal with competition and shifts in demand, a problem that feudal lords never had to worry about. Finally, of course, inheritances are often wasted because the symptoms of grief can undermine an heir's powers of judgment in financial and professional matters.

In spite of preliminary evidence suggesting that a closed aristocracy will not develop in modern America, the critics of inheritance would be justified in calling for increased estate taxes if they could convince the government that they would increase the pace or degree of mobility. They would also be justified if they could convince the government that the redistribution of the wealth of the richest Americans would improve the situation of the middle class and the poor.

At the same time, though, we must recognize that increased estate taxes will not provide sufficient revenue to fully achieve this aim. During the 1950s and 1960s, when only the first $60,000 of an inheritance was tax-exempt, total estate and gift taxes never totaled more than 2 percent of total tax revenue in any year.[13] Due to the 1981 tax reforms, they now constitute 1 percent of the total. So tampering with the estate tax rates will not have a substantial impact on the distribution of wealth. Any serious attempt to redistribute wealth would require a reworking of the entire regulatory framework.

We must remember, though, that public regulation, whatever form it takes, cannot result in the confiscation of private property. So if the government decided that, among other measures, higher inheritance taxes had to be levied to support the goal of general prosperity, it could not impose a tax burden that would, in effect, appropriate an estate. The line that separates legitimate taxation from appropriation would have to be settled by the court system. And a recent Supreme Court decision that seems to elevate inheritance to the status of a natural right addresses this very issue.[14]

# The Supreme Court on Inheritance

For more than 40 years, the Court held to the view that the state had the power to appropriate inherited wealth.[15] Yet in the recent case of *Hodel v. Irving*, the Court took an entirely different position. *Hodel* dealt with the issue of whether the federal government could abolish the inheritance of lands on a Sioux reservation. The land in question had been assigned to individual members of a tribe by the federal government in the late 19th century and then held in a public trust, from which it could not be sold. The aim of this scheme was to ensure that the land would always remain in the hands of Native Americans. However, the Sioux practice of naming multiple heirs eventually divided the original tracts among so many owners that each person's share was too small to be of any practical use. The income accruing from the rental or cultivation of each share was negligible. At the same time, the public cost of administering lands grew as the number of tracts the government had to monitor continually increased.

To deal with these problems, Congress passed the Indian Land Consolidation Act in 1983, which stipulated that any shares that had become too small to be profitable would become the property of the tribe. This allowed the tribe to consolidate useless lands and employ them in a rational and productive way, with the resulting income accruing to the benefit of all its members.

Three members whose shares were absorbed by the tribe objected to the legislation on the ground that it offended the Fifth Amendment. The government had appropriated their interests, which were worth around $4,600, for a public purpose without awarding them "just compensation." The Court found in their favor. Writing for the majority, Justice O'Connor held that the state cannot extinguish any one of the bundle of rights that define a property interest. Among those interests, we must count the right to leave property to anyone we choose. Since the act abolished the right of "descent and devise," it brought about an illegal "taking."

In reaching this decision, Justice O'Connor noted that the state has the power to "regulate" this right, presumably by establishing estate taxes and administrative guidelines. But when regulation becomes appropriation, it runs afoul of the constitutional protection of private property.[16] She thereby supported the distinction that we developed in defending a natural right to inherit wealth.

## Elvis and the Constitution: Conclusion

Now, what does the Court's support of our defense of natural right do for the situation of Ms. Lisa Marie Presley? The Constitution, informed by the philosophy that gave rise to it, would have given the state the power to regulate, that is, to tax Ms. Presley's inheritance. The state could have done so to accelerate class mobility or redistribute wealth so that growth would be widely shared. However, it could never have gone so far as to confiscate the estate, because that would have offended Elvis's natural right to transfer his property and Lisa Marie's corresponding right to receive it.

# Endnotes

## Chapter 1: The Inheritance Generation

1    Phillip Longman, *Born to Pay* (Boston: Houghton Mifflin Co., 1987), p. 1.

2    Robert B. Avery and Michael S. Rendall, "Inheritance and Wealth," a paper presented at the Philanthropy Round-table, Nov. 11, 1993, p. 2.

3    The potential for boomers to receive substantial inheritances was greatly increased by the Reagan tax cuts of 1981. They "more than tripled what a person can bequeath without triggering estate taxes, from $175,625 to 600,000—1.2 million for a couple that plans ahead." ("The New Way to Get Rich," *U.S. News and World Report* [May 7, 1990], pp. 29, 35–6.) And they also dropped the top marginal rate on estates from 70 to 55 percent. (*Ibid.*, pp. 35–7.)

4    Kevin Phillips, *Boiling Point* (New York: Random House, 1993), pp. 19–21; Frank Levy and Robert C. Michel, "Are Baby Boomers Selfish?" *American Demographics* (April 1985), p. 39.

5    Greg J. Duncan, Timothy M. Smeeding, Willard Rodgers, "The Incredible Shrinking Middle Class," *American Demographics* (May 1992), p. 36.

6    Phillips, pp. 7, 23–4.

7    Frank Levy and Robert C. Michel, *The Economic Future of American Families* (Washington, D.C.: Urban Institute Press, 1991), p. 54.

### Chapter 2: The Dangers of Unresolved Grief

1    J. William Worden, *Grief Counselling and Grief Therapy* (New York: Springer Publishing Co., 1982), p. 23.

2    Worden, p. 23; Catherine M. Sanders, *Grief: The Mourning After* (New York: John Wiley and Sons, 1989), pp. 41–2.

3    Worden, p. 22.

4    Worden, pp. 21–2.

5    Worden, p. 27; Colin Murray Parkes, *Bereavement* (London and New York: Tavistock Publications, 1986), pp. 53–5; Lynn Caine, *Being a Widow* (New York: Penguin Books, 1990), pp. 77–8.

6    Erich Lindemann, "Symptomatology and Management of Acute Grief" in Lindemann, *Beyond Grief* (New York: Jason Aronson, 1979), p. 63.

7    Worden, p. 24.

8    Lindemann, pp. 62–3.

9    Worden, p. 22.

10   Parkes maintains that pining, not depression or sadness, is the leading feature of grief and that it appears in the form of "pangs of grief," which he defines as "episodes of severe anxiety and psychological pain." (Parkes, p. 60.) At these times, "lost people are strongly missed and the survivors sob or cry aloud for them." (*Ibid.*, p. 60.) Parkes argues that pining is based on an instinctive survival need, also observed in animals, to search for a lost object (of affection). (*Ibid.*, p. 61.) Searching presupposes the lost object can still be found and in this way operates as a form of denial to cushion us from the full blow of the loss. (*Ibid.*, pp. 94–6.) Restless overactivity, first presented as a symptom by Lindemann, seems to be equated by Parkes with this instinctive pining-searching reaction. (Lindemann, p. 67.) He stresses, though, that insofar as this searching activity is instinctive, we are not aware of our overactivity as an attempt to find the deceased. (Parkes, pp. 94–6; Ira Glick, Robert Weiss, Colin Murray Parkes, *The*

*First Year of Bereavement* [New York: John Wiley and Sons, 1974], p. 8.)

11  Worden, p. 21.

12  Parkes, pp. 99–100.

13  Worden, p. 21.

14  Worden, p. 21; Lindemann, pp. 62–3; Katherine Donnelly, *Recovering From the Loss of a Parent* (New York: Berkley Publishing Company, 1993), p. 33.

15  Parkes, pp. 103–4.

16  Donnelly, p. 40.

17  Donnelly, p. 13.

18  Dr. Mary L.S. Vachon, R.N., Ph.D., "Parental Grief and the Death of a Dream," paper presented at the Annual Meeting of the Canadian Child and Adolescent Psychiatrists Association, St. John's, Newfoundland, Sept. 19, 1989, p. 13.

19  Worden, pp. 11–12.

20  Colin Murray Parkes and Robert S. Weiss, *Recovery From Bereavement* (New York: Basic Books, 1983), pp. 156–7.

21  Worden, p. 13; Donnelly, p. 19; Parkes and Weiss, p. 157.

22  Parkes and Weiss, p. 158.

23  Worden, pp. 14–15; Donnelly, p. 19; Parkes and Weiss, pp. 160–1.

24  Worden, p. 15–16; and 1991 edition, p. 17.

25  Worden, pp. 11–12; Caine, p. 232.

26  Caine, p. 20; Parkes, p. 27.

27  Lindemann, p. 64.

28  Glen W. Davidson, *Understanding Mourning* (Minneapolis: Augsburg Publishing House, 1984), pp. 15–16.

29  Parkes and Weiss, pp. 65–9; Caine, pp. 23–4.

30  Worden, p. 16; Parkes and Weiss, p. 168.

31  Donnelly, p. 39; Worden, p. 25.

32  Worden, p. 24; Davidson, p. 12.

33  Caine, p. 78.

34  Parkes, pp. 55–6; Caine, p. 78.

35  Worden, p. 22; Caine, p. 78.

36  Davidson, pp. 12–13; Donnelly, p. 28.

37  Caine, p. 30.
38  Donnelly, p. 144.
39  Worden, pp. 39–45.
40  Davidson, pp. 79–80.
41  Worden, p. 16.
42  Davidson, pp. 78–9.
43  Caine, p. 41.
44  Dr. Selby Jacobs, Pathologic Grief (Washington, D.C.: American Psychiatric Press, 1993), p. 351.
45  Donnelly, p. 81.
46  Worden, p. 59; Lindemann, pp. 69, 70; Donnelly, pp. 81–2.
47  Donnelly, pp. 82, 208–9.
48  Lindemann, p. 67.
49  Worden, p. 59; Donnelly, p. 82.
50  Worden, p. 59.
51  Jacobs, pp. 59, 350; Donnelly, p. 83.
52  Parkes and Weiss, pp. 131–2, 153–4, 171.
53  See the example of Betty Farnsworth in Chapter 5.
54  Parkes and Weiss, pp. 21, 153.
55  Parkes and Weiss, pp. 65–9, 94–5, 171.
56  Jacobs, p. 178.
57  Worden, p. 59; Donnelly, p. 82.
58  Parkes and Weiss, p. 52.
59  Lindemann, p. 71.
60  Lindemann, p. 70.
61  Lindemann, p. 71.
62  Worden, pp. 93–4.
63  Parkes and Weiss, pp. 94–5.
64  Parkes, p. 57.
65  Erich Lindemann, "Grief and Grief Management: Some Reflections," Journal of Pastoral Care (Sept. 1976), Vol. XXX, No. 3, p. 205.
66  Worden, p. 44.

## Chapter 3: The Syndromes of Grief

1  Glen W. Davidson, Understanding Mourning (Minneapolis: Augsburg Publishing House, 1984), pp. 16–17.

2   Lisa Gubernick, "That's My Excuse, Anyway," *Forbes 400* (October 28, 1985), p. 50.

## Chapter 4: The Syndromes of Affluence

1   The Inheritance Project, "The Inheritor's Inner Landscape," p. 16.
2   Jaclyn Fierman, "Great Fortunes Lost," *Fortune* (July 18, 1988), p. 81.
3   Fierman, p. 79.
4   "2 Sons Contest $84 million Cafritz Will," *Washington Post* (June 30, 1989), p. A1.
5   "2 Sons", *Post*, p. A1; Marjorie Williams, "Cafritz v. Cafritz," *Washington Post Magazine* (February 25, 1990), pp. 18, 35.
6   Williams, p. 18.
7   "2 sons," *Post*, pp. A1, A16; Williams, p. 18.
8   Williams, pp. 16–21, 32, 36.

## Chapter 5: How to Give and Take Bad Advice

1   C.B. Wortman and D.R. Lehman, "Reactions to Victims of Life Crisis: Support Attempts that Fail" in I.G. Sarason and B.R. Sarason, eds., *Social Support: Theory, Research and Applications* (Dordrecht, The Netherlands: Martinus Nijhoff, 1985), pp. 464–6.
2   Dr. Mary L.S. Vachon, R.N., Ph.D., "Parental Grief and the Death of a Dream," paper presented at the annual meeting of the Canadian Child and Adolescent Psychiatrists Association, St. John's Newfoundland, Sept. 19, 1989, p. 13. See also Mary Vachon and Stanley Stylianos, "The Role of Social Support in Bereavement," *Journal of Social Issues* (1988), Vol. 44, No. 3, pp. 180–2.
3   Wortman and Lehman, pp. 472, 475.
4   I am indebted to William Dimitroff, a partner with the law firm of Meighen Demers in Toronto, for this idea.
5   Communities have been weakened because their members are constantly changing and their beliefs and traditions are eroding under the influence of competing values.

## Chapter 6: Family Conflicts

1   J. William Worden, *Grief Counselling and Grief Therapy* (New York: Springer Publishing Co., 1982), pp. 97–8; Elliott J. Rosen, *Families Facing Death* (Lexington, Mass.: Lexington Books, 1990), p. 18.

2   Rosen, p. 18.

3   Rosen, p. 98.

4   Catherine M. Sanders, *Grief: The Mourning After* (New York: John Wiley and Sons, 1989), p. 151.

5   Lois F. Akner, *How to Survive the Loss of a Parent* (New York: William Morrow, 1993), p. 143.

6   Worden, pp. 97–9, 104.

7   Sanders, p. 149.

8   Sanders, p. 150; Edward Myers, *When Parents Die* (New York: Penguin Books, 1987), p. 135.

9   Andrea Gross, "The Last Taboo," *Ladies' Home Journal* (April 1990), p. 144.

10   Michael Waldholz, "Trial Begins Over $400 Million Estate of Son of Johnson & Johnson's Founder," *The Wall Street Journal* (February 28, 1986), p. 6.

11   Waldholz, p. 6; Joyce Hoffman, "The Way of a Will," *Washington Post Magazine* (Jan. 19, 1986), p. 8; Reuter, "Settlement Reached on J. Seward Johnson Will," *Washington Post* (June 3, 1986), p. D2; United Press International, "The Widow's Cinderella Castle," *Washington Post* (June 5, 1986), p. C3.

12   Hoffman, p. 17.

13   Hoffman, pp. 8, 16, 17; Waldholz, p. 6; Reuter, p. D2.

14   Gross, p. 148.

15   "Complex Will Leaves Tangled Web," *Washington Post* (July 14, 1985), p. C5.

16   Richard J. Kirkland Jr., "Should You Leave It," *Fortune* (September 29, 1986), p. 22.

17   Kirkland, pp. 18, 22.

18   Kirkland, p. 22.

19   Andrew Erdman, "The Billionaires," *Fortune* (September 10, 1990), p. 122.

20   Rosen, p. 92.

²¹ Sanders, p. 157.
²² Therese A. Rando, *How To Go On Living When Someone You Love Dies* (New York: Bantam Books, 1988), p. 125.
²³ Rando, p. 125.
²⁴ Myers, p. 135.

## Chapter 7: The Value of a Thing

¹ Srully Blotnick, "The Case of the Reluctant Heirs," *Forbes* (July 16, 1984), p. 180; Edward F. Cone, "'Dad, I Know I Can Handle It,'" *Forbes 400* (October 26, 1987), p. 370: "According to academic experts, 70 percent of family businesses fail to survive their founders."

## Chapter 8 :The Meaning of Loss

¹ William Shakespeare, *Hamlet*, Harold Jenkins, ed. (Arden Edition) (London and New York: Routledge, 1992), Act 1, Sc. 2, pp. 129–134.

## Postscript: In Defense of Inheritance

¹ "The Presley Inheritance," *People Magazine* (March 1, 1993), pp. 67-70.

² Alexander Hamilton, James Madison and John Jay, *The Federalist Papers* (New York: New American Library, 1961), p. 78.

³ Two of the most popular theories are utilitarianism and positivism. Utilitarian theories give the legislature the freedom to vote against the guarantee of any right as long as it is satisfied that doing so will improve the welfare of the majority. If, for instance, the legislature is satisfied that a decree authorizing the confiscation of the property of a minority group is in the majority's interest, the decree is just. There is no constitutional restraint on the government's regulation of property. The right to inherit can legitimately be nullified by the government. Positivistic theories lead to much the same result. They hold that as long as the government has passed laws in accordance with the proper procedures—for instance, a traditional or constitutional requirement of a majority vote in the legislature—those laws are binding on the

citizenry. Thus, a law that gives the government a claim over the property of its citizens, including inherited property, is just if it has been passed using the proper procedures.

Legal scholars who wished to find a convincing justification for defending natural rights have sought refuge in a new liberal philosophy proposed by Harvard professor John Rawls, in his 1971 treatise entitled *A Theory of Justice*. Rawls has become a mainstay of courses in legal philosophy because he promises the best of both worlds. He claims to restore the framers' notion that the purpose of government is to guarantee fundamental rights yet does so working from the modern premise that we are not naturally endowed with these rights.

Rawls begins with the assumption that the people have a right to choose the rules that will govern their association. The problem, though, is that these rules can be regarded as just only if they are chosen under conditions that are fair. And fairness means that everyone must judge impartially or objectively. No one should choose rules simply to promote selfish aims, which include protecting his existing social and financial privileges. He argues that the only way to achieve this impartial standpoint is to imagine that we must choose the rules without knowing anything about our innate or acquired advantages. We must somehow forget who we are.

Apparently, the first thing that we would agree on if we could achieve this state is that we do not have an absolute right to our innate talents (they are accidents of birth and circumstance). We would also agree that we don't have an absolute right to our possessions because they are products of our talents. And since we don't deserve our talents, we certainly can't own what results from exercising them. If our property came from inheritance, we also couldn't have an absolute right to it. Since we don't have an absolute right to what we create by our own effort and creativity, we can't have an absolute right to property that is simply dumped in our laps. All this means that the ownership and distribution of property, including inheritable property, is determined by a public vote.

So, how would we vote, assuming for a moment that each person in a society could somehow forget who he or she was and what he or she owned? Rawls argues that each of us would have to consider that he might end up in the position of a disadvantaged person after he has chosen the rules and regained knowledge of himself. That forces each of us to vote for two basic rules that protect both the majority and minority. The first is that each person must be guaranteed basic rights such as life, liberty and the pursuit of happiness. This principle, although reminiscent of the Constitution, does not contain a right to private property. The distribution of property is determined by Rawls's second principle, which holds that social and economic goods must be distributed equally unless an unequal distribution would improve everyone's situation, including that of the disadvantaged. (John Rawls, *A Theory of Justice* [Cambridge: Harvard University Press, 1971], pp. 3, 7, 12, 14, 15, 18, 60, 120, 137, 180.)

On the one hand, guided by this principle, we might vote to abolish inheritance. Each of us, imagining that he might end up in a disadvantaged family that has nothing to transmit, would fail to see any point in securing a right to receive a bequest. A right to inherit would not make the least advantaged better off. On the other hand, everyone might vote to secure the right believing that the situation of the least advantaged might be adversely affected by the expropriation of estates. It might lead to a flight of capital from the country, or discourage savings and reduce the availability of investment capital, thereby causing a general economic decline that might punish the poor even more than the rich. Rawls' theory is so far from establishing private property as a fundamental right that it issues in two contradictory views on the status of the right to inherit.

[4]  Thomas L. Pangle, *The Spirit of Modern Republicanism* (Chicago: The University of Chicago Press, 1988), pp. 125–7.

[5]  John Locke, *Two Treatises of Government* (New York: New American Library, 1965), Book II, para. 6, 25–51, 72–3, 120, 139–142, 184.

[6]  Locke, para. 65; Pangle, pp. 233, 237–9.

7  Leo Strauss, *Natural Right And History* (Chicago: University of Chicago Press, 1953), pp. 235-6, 238-9.

8  Kevin Phillips, *The Politics of Rich and Poor* (New York: Random House, 1990), pp. 12, 14.

9  Maureen A. Maloney, "Distributive Justice: That Is the Wealth Tax Issue," University of Ottawa Law Review (1984), Vol. 20, p. 603.

10  Phillips, pp. 10–12, 14, 157–166. Also note that the fear of a new aristocracy is compounded by statistics suggesting that estate taxes have had little effect on reducing the impact of inheritance. The 1981 tax reform, which phased in a $600,000 exemption that rose to $1.2 million for a couple, reduced the group of taxable decedents from 10 percent to 3 percent. (Note that some believe the real figure is less than 1 percent.) The tax itself also had a diminishing impact due to a reduction in the top rate, which applied only to estates worth $10 million or more, from 70 percent to 55 ("The New Way to Get Rich," pp. 35–6; Michael Graetz, "To Praise the Estate Tax, Not To Bury It," Yale Law Journal [1983], Vol. 93, pp. 259, 262–3) and the loopholes that permeate the tax code. (Mark L. Ascher, "Curtailing Inherited Wealth," Michigan Law Review [1990], Vol. 89, pp. 69, 72.) Currently, the top rate kicks in at $3 million.

11  Lester Thurow, Generating Inequality (New York: Basic Books, 1976), pp. 129–30; D.W. Haslett, "Is Inheritance Justified?" Philosophy and Public Affairs (Spring 1986), 125–6; Sidney L. Carroll, "American Family Fortunes as Economic Deadweight," *Challenge* (May-June 1991), p. 13.

12  Jaclyn Fierman, "Great Fortunes Lost," *Fortune* (July 18, 1988), p. 76.

13  Graetz, pp. 265–6.

14  *Hodel v. Irving* 481 U.S. 704 (1987); Ronald Chester, "Essay: Is the Right to Devise Property Constitutionally Protected?—The Strange Case of *Hodel v. Irving*," *Southwestern University Law Review* (1995), Vol. 24, p. 1195.

15  314 U.S. 556, 562 (1942).

16  *Hodel v. Irving*, pp. 716–7.

# About
# the Author

Michael Alexander understands the human dimensions
of inheritance because he has lived them. At the age of 19,
he became the principal administrator of a family investment trust and held the position for 16 years. In that role,
he had to deal with all the issues and problems that are
addressed in *How to Inherit Money*. Among his many experiences, he hired and fired professionals, had his co-
trustees dismissed for negligence, received disastrous advice from friends, chased missing funds in foreign countries, uncovered fraud and theft, fought major tax battles
with Revenue Canada, bought and sold objects through
major auction houses, made and lost large sums of money,
and witnessed the passing of every member of his family
due to illness and misfortune.

Mr. Alexander holds law degrees from Columbia University and the University of Toronto and has studied philosophy and political science at the graduate level at both schools. At Toronto, he obtained a Bachelor's degree in political science and a Master's degree in political philosophy, working under the direction of the late Allan Bloom, author of the best-selling book, *The Closing of the American Mind*. In 1985 and 1986, he was named a Laidlaw Fellow in Law and Political Science at U of T. He has also been a visiting scholar at the Committee on Social Thought at the University of Chicago and l'Institut d'Etudes Politiques in Paris. He is a Member of the Bar of Ontario and has several years of experience as a consultant in the field of trusts and estates. He is also a partner in Ion Productions, a company that creates articles, books and films.

Michael Alexander can be reached at Station F, Box 973, Toronto, Ontario, Canada  M4Y 2N9.

# Index